CONTENTS

FOREWORD

I am extremely honoured to write the foreword of *The Job I called a Dream* for many reasons, first and foremost, I have been an entrepreneur for close to 20 years. Out of all the books I've read on the subject of business productivity and skill ability, this book hits the nail on the head on what it takes to truly be successful in a fast-paced business world.

I certainly say that focus is the most vital element when it comes to being a successful business owner; as Ryan describes in his incredible book. The moment I focused on the most important aspects of my business and high leverage activities, my business exponentially grew.

I had to learn how to say no more than I said yes, and I stopped doing low leverage tasks and avoided shiny objects.

Ryan is the epitome of a focused entrepreneur. I had the pleasure of coaching him, and from that very moment he started my program, he made tremendous gains in his personal and professional life, and one of the reasons is because his level of focus is uncanny.

He gets stuff done and does not get distracted by shiny objects. His focus also allows him to have a balanced life, not just successful business, but also a fulfilled family life and thriving bodybuilding career.

Ryan is the go-to guy when it comes to learning about this subject, and you will get so much out of "The Job I called a Dream."

I've actually read it twice because there are so many gems and nuggets to be applied. I highly suggest that you read it once just to take in information, and then read it a second time and create an action plan so you can put his amazing content into play.

What you learn from the information in this book will bring you not only the skills you need to make your business prosper, but you will acquire more freedom and fulfilment as well. Be sure to gift this book to as many people as possible, the words contained in this work of art will transform many lives.

AJ Mihrzad,
Founder of OnlineSupercoach.com

INTRODUCTION

I'm Ryan Hodgson, and I'm a fitness business owner and entrepreneur, but my first and most important job is being a husband and a father. Something I've only learnt on my journey about prioritising family.

When I was younger, I think I always struggled to stay focused on things. Particularly when I didn't enjoy it as much, I lose interest and ultimately become a nightmare to those around me. However, I've always had a strong mind, and when I knew I wanted to do something, that was all I could focus on.

I think this is what made me good when it comes to running a business and when it comes to building up the clientele and keeping them going even when things don't seem to be going 100% right. Without that sort of attitude, it's safe to say I'd probably be back working in a job that I didn't enjoy counting down the hours, minutes, and seconds till I finished work.

I've always had a strong passion for health and fitness and I decided to write this book just a few days after I sold my first successful business, which was Fit Body Jersey. It was the first 'proper' business I had that turned over multiple six figures a year. I want this book to give people an insight into the harsh reality that I found when I started up on my own.

I want it to help people see a little bit more of the challenges and struggles that the entrepreneur faces. I used to watch videos, read books, look at blogs of entrepreneurs everywhere and they always painted the same glamorous lifestyle:

The wads of cash

The fancy cars

The nice clothes

The bling everywhere,

It was something I really wanted and longed for, something being honest I felt I should have. Why not? Nevertheless, it was only when I decided to go for it myself and work hard towards that dream lifestyle, did I start to see what really lied beneath the surface of these ideal lifestyles.

The pressure it puts on me, the pressure it puts on my family, and the pressure it puts on the friendships and relationships around me. Therefore, I decided to write this, so that people who read it can have a greater understanding and go into running their own businesses with their eyes open. Something I wish I had before I started because it would have saved me a lot of heartache, and a lot of time too (and probably less grey hairs).

I want to make it clear from the offset, that I am nothing special; I don't have any high qualifications or any extremely rare talent. In fact I used to be a quitter to quit anything I didn't take my hand to like, college, and my time in the army for example. Now I'm just a hard working bloke that's learnt things along the way and I hope this can help you on your journey too without making the same mistakes I have.

An overnight success

I'm a big believer that there is no such thing as an overnight success. It comes from years and years of hard work, lessons, and often mistakes or failures for you to learn the recipes to see success. Consistency is key when it comes to true success because if it doesn't last, can you really call it a success? I'm not somebody who thinks of myself as successful yet, however, I have come on the path to learning more and more lessons as I go on in life.

Only when you start to address the lessons, mistakes and failures, and take actions based on them can you start to become a real success. When we see these people painting the overnight success stories of selling their coaching, give them money and they'll make you an overnight success, it does frustrate me. Because, in a society where people are desperate, they want that overnight success. And I want the overnight success too, but I'm not afraid to admit that I want to be a success tomorrow. However, the last few years have really taught me that it will take time.

I don't want this book to come across all doom and gloom because there are a lot of pros to operating and running your own business. I'm fortunate enough right now that I have paid myself very well since becoming self-employed and building up a business.

I have had some great holidays, I had my dream wedding, I live my dream where we have a nice car and live in a nice house. However, I just want to remove the blinkers because I know it's so easily done. You see shiny objects and you think that it's easy. There are many challenges in place and I want people to see both sides to operating your own business.

We seem to be in a culture now where everyone seems to think they're a business coach promising you the world, six figures or even seven in 90 days, and generate 100 clients in 10 days. All of these various things that sound attractive are again shiny object syndrome that I think most new entrepreneurs' experience.

I'm not a business coach, yet (still got a lot to learn) and don't pretend to be, that's not my passion right now. To be clear, my passion is in helping people lose weight and feel better about themselves, I just happened to have set up a few companies and learnt a few things on the way that I want to share.

I've just based this book on my own personal experience and hope that I can help people open their eyes, remove the blinkers, and forget the shiny object, or the cash chasing and grow their own business in a way that they won't make the same mistakes I did, because I hate admitting mistakes but I've made them and cannot pretend that I haven't.

I want people to see these mistakes and hope that less people will make them in the future; meaning they can run their own businesses that fit their lifestyle in a way that they'd imagined it would work.

How it All Began

Thus, at the beginning, I never knew what I wanted to do. Truth be told, I was probably one of the most unruly children at school and jumped from job to job when I left school. Working at Marks and Spencer's, the Army, back to Marks and Spencer's, and then I even got a job in the bank.

I soon realised that sitting in an office really wasn't for me either. After giving it a long, hard thought, I realised that I needed to do something that was going to fulfil my passion of training. I was a boxer for the local boxing club at the time and I also thought that I needed to use my energy levels because I felt like I had so much to burn.

Therefore, I thought this would be something that would be perfect for me. I spent some time looking up information about personal training and realised the costs involved. I soon realised that trying to pay for the personal training course alongside my rent, my bills, etc., was going to be tough.

This led me to go back to the thing that I knew best, which was Marks and Spencer. They gave me a job working Monday to Saturday, 5:00 a.m. to 8:00 a.m., which meant that I could still keep my job in the bank as well.

Feeling absolutely wiped out after a few months, I finally had enough saved to do the personal training course and I went for it. I went through the European Institute of Fitness and the course I did was great, I really enjoyed it and felt it gave me the knowledge I needed.

I always thought from that moment on it was going to get easy. However, I couldn't be more wrong, in fact the hard work was really only about to start.

When I came back from my personal training course, reality hit me that the bills didn't stop while I was away, I just didn't have income while I was away studying.

Then, telling anyone who would listen that I was a qualified Personal Trainer, I soon realised that people didn't want to train with me just because I'd qualified because the truth was; it doesn't really mean a lot until I backed it up. I had to go out there and prove myself, which then led me on to the next challenges I faced when I decided to join Fitness First.

When I did my personal training course, I decided to do it through a company that was probably the most expensive at the time. I did it online where I studied for 10 weeks at home and then went away for 10 days of assessments and a sort of a recap of everything we'd learned.

I have to say that until those 10 days, I didn't have a clue about most of the things involved in the course because I wasn't very good with self-studying and I struggled with that. However, going on the course, those 10 days I did felt as if I learnt loads in such a short space of time. I learnt so much about the human body, its movements, its muscles, and its energy systems, pretty much everything you needed to know to be a personal trainer.

I also learned about different training programs, how to train people. One thing they didn't really teach and I found it really surprising was how to get clients. How to find clients, and what to do to keep a hold on them. This is something that I left my PT course thinking would be easy but how wrong I was.

Although I do fully agree it's important to know a lot about the human body and different training methods, I also think it's extremely important to understand a little bit more about client relations and contacting clients as well as how to gain clients because we are in a society where there's a lot of young people investing their hard earned money to become personal trainers and struggling because it is an extremely competitive market.

There are many trainers out there doing the exact same thing, going on the course that shows them 'text book' coaching, and reality is far from this. They leave their course with a qualification and realise that they're not sure how to get clients. I actually think these courses should include something a little bit more related to how to get clients and maintain them once you've got them, because it really becomes common sense after time; you can waste a lot of time and effort trying to learn this.

Often this is why there are so many good trainers not quite making it because they're struggling to maintain their client base to live -- to be able to afford to live (and in reality they probably saw the same wads of cash and the fancy cars I did).

Personal Trainer on my Back

Straight after I qualified as a personal trainer, the first thing I did was contact Fitness First, which was the most popular gym in Jersey. When I went to see them, the Health and Fitness Manager there ran through all of the various options that I would get if I was to come and work there as a self-employed personal trainer. I always remember seeing all the trainers in there with their sparkly uniforms and the words 'personal trainer' on their back; I really, really wanted to do that.

I went away with all of these options to weigh up, with a mixture of emotions, excited, nervous, confused, and being honest absolutely, bricking it. I sat down, looked at my bank balances, my credit card balances, my loans and my out goings, and soon began to think that being a personal trainer was just a fucking dream and it was never going to be a reality. I had to decline the offer based on my personal finances, as it was too big of a risk to take at the time.

A few weeks later, one of the lads that I used to box with approached me, Harry McClinton, and we talked about an idea of a business we had. I decided to go with him for a chat at Fitness First, where Mark Stewart decided to give me option of doing a sliding scale. I jumped on the opportunity, because it gave me 12 weeks to gradually build the rent I paid the gym up, which also gave me 12 weeks to get my client base up to enough training to cover my rent and hopefully the bills, so that I could leave my Job at Marks and Spencer.

I thought that it was going to be easy. I was in for a real shock. After the twelve weeks, my rent was up to 160 pounds a week. I was currently being paid for three sessions a week, which was 105 pounds a week at the time. So, I was actually losing 55 pounds a week before I even start to pay my bills anywhere else.

Luckily, I had always kept my job at Mark's and Spencer in the mornings, which just about kept me treading water so to speak. That, along with a couple of credit cards I had at the time with 'free balance transfers' which helped me cover all the bills.

In fact, I even wrote a letter to hand in my resignation at Fitness First after just 13 weeks of being there. However, something clicked one day and I had two clients who decided to train with me; both of them for twice a week, I'll never forget them, Joanne Le Bihan and Sandra Lee. My personal training income just doubled in a day, and I was feeling more positive.

I then decided that I just needed to keep working at it, and it wasn't going to come easy. I started to talk to the management at the gym about doing classes, and doing other things to try to help raise my profile in the gym. I started to learn a little bit more about how to gain more patrons from the clients that I have and how to keep hold of the clients I had. I remember watching Wayne Stewart, who is now my personal trainer, and how he was with his clients thinking, 'I want to be like that,' it was no surprise he was fully booked.

No one had prepared me for how tough it was going to be working for myself, the sleepless nights, the countless number of hours I sat there working out how I was going to get through the next month. How I was going to be able to put food on the table for myself. Luckily, I was a single man; otherwise, I would have never been able to do it.

When I was struggling at Fitness First to pay the bills and cover the rent,I still tried to spend every spare moment I had in the gym. I would go there straight after my Marks and Spencer job and stay there until I was doing my job on the doors at night. I stayed in there to interact with the members, with the other personal trainers, and with the staff of the gym.

I helped in reception when I could because it meant I have to meet all of the clients first hand and introduce myself. I also got to know the sales team and then became friends with one of the sales girls who really helped me to grow my client-base over time. She sent the right clients my way, people she knew I would connect with and she's already sold me to them.

She really helped me out to get my business off, up and running. From that day on, which I will always remember that sometimes it's not necessarily what you know it's about who you know and knowing the right people, the people that will help and support you is what is going to make it a lot easier. I always used to have a sense of pride and hate asking for help. However, now I know that the proudest thing you can do is not to admit when you need help, something that is going to stay with me forever. I always ask for help whenever I need it now.

After being at Fitness First for about four months, I spoke to the Health and Fitness manager once again about various options that I had to help me cover my rent through doing things like classes, although at the time I would have cleaned the gym if it were an option. But the reality was that I only had my personal training course qualification, which meant there were only a few classes I could do, and the trainers that had been there longer than me were already taking these.

After a little bit of negotiations, they agreed to pay for my spinning course, which I could repay by doing classes when I got back. That was a great opportunity for me because I knew that when I got back I could do enough classes to cover my rent. In addition, it meant that anything else I made from my personal training was mine to cover my bills, etc.

I will never forget my first group training class. I was ready about an hour before it started in the studio, absolutely bricking it because it was really out of my comfort zone. Before this, I was hiding within a comfort zone of just training one to ones and only really stuck with things that I was comfortable with so that it was easier for me to work. I guess you could say that I lacked confidence in what I was doing at the start.

By doing these group classes and starting them, I definitely found my confidence improved, not only with the group stuff, but also with my one-to-ones and also in general, life. It was a massive change. So I really learned quite early on in my career to push myself out of my comfort zone.

It's worth mentioning at this time I was still working at Mark and Spencer's that I had also started working on the doors in the evenings. After about three months of doing these classes, working at Marks and Spencer's and working on the door, I decided that enough was enough.

I had no life, I wasn't seeing any of my friends, and I was constantly tired, moody and just generally fed up. All that kept me at it was the thought perhaps, if I give it another few months, I'll double my income again. I'll double it again and again. I gave it some time.I walked away from the gym that night and took my frustrations out on the bags at the boxing gym, then pondered on it for a few weeks. I then realised that this is what I wanted to do.

I really wanted to help as many people as I could get in shape and that was my ultimate goal, and that wasn't something I was about to give up on too easily.

I had to go through all of this because if I didn't, I faced the reality of working in retail or working in the bank; and there is nothing wrong with this, but it's not just for me. It's not something I enjoyed.

So, fast-forward about six months, I'd been working in Fitness First for just over a year, and I was fully booked as a personal trainer. I'd say from month five to month 12, I learned more about myself than I thought was possible at the time. The challenges I faced becoming a personal trainer, the challenges I faced being self-employed and realising that I wasn't just a personal trainer;

I was my own bookkeeper,

I was my own administrator

I was my own manager,

I was my own receptionist,

I was basically my everything.

I soon realised that I have to wear many hats just to function as a business. That became a challenge. I'd finish my days training clients and then spend the day getting back to people who had emailed me, asking for tips on food; it was constant.

After a few months of me getting busier and busier, I started to notice that certain people within the gym environment weren't talking to me anymore without any explanation. The only thing I could think of was perhaps they were a little bit jealous that I had started to gain more clients, which was strange; I was there literally around the clock talking to everyone while they went home for naps and partied all weekend and took till Wednesday to recover.

I did notice that the trainers in there that were busier were always very nice and always helping out other trainers, yet the ones that were quiet didn't want to talk to me.

That was a lesson I learned earlier on; sometimes the people who are higher up help other people on the way up too. Those that are at the bottom or not doing so well want to try to drag the others down with them. A lesson really worth remembering, if you're going into being self-employed because it can sometimes get you down.

I used to blame myself, and question if I had done something to upset them, it was only a couple of years later that the issues they had, were with themselves and not with me.

However, I realised that the only way I could do it was to keep going.

The Phone Call that Changed my Life

One day, I got a phone call from a number that I didn't know. Once I answered it, I found out that it was Craig Culkin, someone that I knew of and looked up to in the fitness industry; he was also the best boxer in Jersey at the time too, plus the fact that he was Jersey's football manager. So he had quite a high profile role in the Island.

He asked me if I could meet him at the Radisson Hotel where he was based on lunchtime for a chat. I jumped at a chance to go and meet him, confused as to what he wanted to talk to me about, and really unsure of what to expect. I hadn't played football for years. I had hardly spoken to him at the gym either. When I went to meet him, he told me he was going away for a few days and needed someone to cover his boxing classes.

We had a little discussion about money. I bumped him up to pay me a little bit more than what he wanted, but was also a little bit more than the minimum I would have taken. I was happy. I didn't let him know that at the time. Then while he was away, he gave me another phone call and told me that he was in the states at a Fitness Summit and wanted to know if I was interested in a business opportunity.

Even when I got phone call from Craig about setting up a business together, I knew straight away that I wanted to do it; however, I did have one thing in my mind. I was in the process of setting up a business with my friend, Harry McClinton, and we were going to set our own company Hotshots. In this business, we were going to run various group training sessions and basically set them up ourselves and they would have been very similar to what Fit Body was. I told harry before we told anyone else because I thought I owed it to him to let him know in advance that I was no longer going to run the business with him and was going to set up with Craig. A tough thing to do. However, definitely the right thing to do too.

Before Craig rang me and got me to research Fit Body Boot Camp, I was relatively naive about the fitness industry.

I honestly thought that personal training was the be all and end all of health and fitness. Pulling in over £1,000 a week. At the time, I was 22 years old, and was happy with that. I thought that doing group training was just something that people do to help pay the bills if they needed it. Because that was all I had done at the time, when I was struggling at the start I picked up a few classes to pay the bills. I was really happy, and was earning a good wage. In fact, I was earning a lot more than I ever thought I would.

Then, after having my eyes opened about Fit Body Boot Camp and group training, I started to realise how much more potential there was. How much more money I could earn, probably worth saying at this time how much more people I could help was only a secondary thought, wrong from the very start. I also began to realise how much more of a business it could become, rather than just a one-man band or a soul person business. I knew that I was on the fast learning curve, and I knew I'd have to keep up the pace because anything that does well will inevitably be open to being copied one way or another.

I jumped at the chance and said yes, I'd love to hear more. He told me about a franchise called Fit Body Boot camp, and asked me to do some research before he got home. That night, I spent the whole evening e-mailing and texting all of the Fit Body Boot camp owners in the UK. Once I'd done that, I arranged to speak to pretty much all of them in the UK to find out more information about how it operates, what to expect from it, and how we'd go about setting up our own.

When Craig returned, we had a little chat together and a brief discussion with the owner of Fit Body Boot camp about the franchise. After we'd found out a little bit more about the costs involved, I have to admit that I had a lot of doubts in my mind, because it was me using yet another credit card, maxing out a credit card just so I could set this business up. However, my gut told me not to question it. The amount of fear rushing through my body at the time of what if it doesn't work, how am I going to pay these bills, I was losing clients as it is by trying to do all these classes around clients and asking people to juggle everything around me.

It was a struggle. I decided that Craig was the person that would make it work, if anyone was going to make it work. Therefore, I agreed to do it and maxed my credit card out. I didn't tell him this at the time of my financial struggles.

Getting the Franchise

After we paid for the franchise, we then found out that we had to go away there to do a course; a five-day course in California, which we decided to make into a 10-day tour. Something that was really exciting to me because I'd never been to America, but also something that I absolutely freaked out about because it meant more debt.

A few weeks later, I told my clients that I was just going away to see family for 10 days. Craig had also done the same, which meant we had to keep things quiet so that no one knew what we were up to. We even saw a local businessman that we both knew personally and had to sit separately and get our bags alone too before he could put two and two together. We kept everything very quiet while we were planning this. We went on the course, and had a great time.

On the first trip to the States, there were two parts to the course. One of them was theory, and the other one was practical. On the theory side of it, we learned a lot about the operations and the way that the franchise was built and run. We got to meet everyone at head offices and really got a good opportunity to ask any questions.

It turned out that we were the only two on the theory part of the course, which meant that we had a whole day of one-to-one coaching from Bedros Keullian. This was a great asset, as I know it would've cost a fortune had it not been planned that way.

On the practical side of it, we had been put through workouts and then had to deliver them ourselves. There were more trainers on that, and it was great fun. It was a hard workout, and I got to see how much of an impact Fit Body Jersey was going to make once we'd returned and set it up. I left the course feeling really excited and looking forward to a business that was about to start building.

I did not only see a part of the world that I'd never seen before, and thought I would never see, I fell in love with California straight away. Craig and I managed to make the trip a bit longer than it really had to be so that we could see some of its cruising around California, which we convinced ourselves, was 'vital business work', but we really had an epic time.

For TEN days we worked hard but played hard as well learning all about the franchise and how it operated, and we left there feeling ready to set up once we returned. We also had some very good nights out in Hollywood, Newport Beach (woke up with an unexpected tattoo after that one), and then we even ended up going to Vegas for two nights as well.

When we got to the States, the first thing we did was went to Hollywood. We had a night out in Hollywood, in Suppa Club. It was fucking epic, I'd never been anywhere like it. When we were getting ready, as I started to get dressed, and put on my shirt and trousers, Craig was mortified. I didn't have a blazer. I hadn't brought a blazer with me because it wasn't really something that I wore. I'd never been to the States and didn't really know what to expect. Therefore, Craig got me to wear one of his blazers. I went out that night looking like I was wearing my dad's coat, but I wore the jacket, and it made us both laugh anyway.

That was one of the best trips of my life and it was all for 'work' I'll never forget getting back wanting to tell my mates, but we couldn't because we had agreed to keep it quiet until we announced the launch of Fit Body Jersey.

I had never been away like that before with a friend or somebody who hardly knew me, but we got to see a lot of America. It was a great time. When we got back, the real hard work began, so we were ready to hit the ground running when we launched.

Soon after we decided to go with Fit Body Boot camp, I realised the amount of work and preparation that went into setting up a new business. The amount of meetings you have to go to. The amount of hoops you have to jump through to register the business, set up bank accounts, and make sure that you have the right insurance.

I was just a personal trainer; I didn't expect to have all of this 'admin' before we even started. Then there were the other bits of practical work, like getting the equipment, generating interest and clients involved. It was quite overwhelming at first; I have to admit, 22 years old with what felt like a huge weight on my shoulders.

Craig and I were running around like lunatics for the first few weeks of this preparation phase, just to get everything in place, to make sure that when we started, we were ready to rock and roll, and nothing was going to upset it, or get in the way, it's the first time in my life I had looked ahead to be honest.

We ordered equipment, set up the insurance, spoke to the local school about setting up our boot camps, and the times that we could run them. Then, six weeks before we launched, we decided to announce it so that we could make sure that the boot camps were pretty full when we first started.

We soon started to get a lot of enquiries about our boot camps, as it was a completely new structure to how things were ran in Jersey, other boot camps didn't run 6 days a week and weren't members only.

We sat down and mapped out the classes. We both agreed to make sure that we set the same standard, to run every class together for the first eight weeks. This sounded great, until we started to look at our clients' diaries and realised that it meant that both of us would be taking a massive hit in our personal training income, which added to the fact that we still didn't have a sustainable income in the business before it started, we were taking a massive risk.

In fact, I've got to be honest, I think the more I thought about it, the more I wanted to pull out of this, but I was already balls deep and had invested too much money and time to do this. Therefore, I couldn't really come back. I couldn't let Craig down.

I couldn't be somebody who had given up at the first hurdle because I knew I'd kick myself if he'd got somebody else and then they had done well. So I'd given my clients four weeks' notice. I told them all if they trained anymore in the evening that I'd have to discontinue training them at those times.

Half of them decided to try the boot camps, and some of them decided that it was best to part ways there. This meant that I immediately saw a massive dip in my income, because the ones that moved to boot camp were getting a preferential rate to try it out, and the ones that left, of course, I lost that money.

Before we started up, we managed to get about 15 people, paid in full for the year. They paid £750 up front, which gave us the money we needed to get the business off the ground. We bought the equipment, and the first few months of rent in the bank.

Therefore, we knew we were hitting the ground running from day one. This also minimized the risk of us going there and not making a penny, and having to pay for everything ourselves, because ultimately, you already knew we were both going to be losing money because you have to reduce the amount of personal training sessions we were doing, as we set up and started doing every single session together.

I do have to say I was so surprised that people would spend that for something that hadn't even started yet, even though most of them (15) stayed for more than the first year.

I was stressed, fed up, frustrated, was feeling sick at the thought of the debt that was up to my eyeballs. I struggled. I struggled to keep it together and keep motivated, because I knew that these first eight weeks were so important for us to build a business. However, I knew that there were two of us in it, and I had to get through it. This led me to the start of Fit Body boot camp in our first session.

Fit Body Boot Camp Taking Over

I will never forget the night before we had our session at Haute Vallee School. I didn't sleep a wink. Nervous, anxious, and absolutely bricking it. Unsure of how well done it was going to go. I knew we had plenty of people trialling us; however, they were paying next to nothing and this could have all been a risk not worth taking.

For the first session, I set my alarm for4:00 and met Craig up at the school at 5:00. We spent an hour setting things up, getting things organised, so we were ready to take the sessions together.

Craig was the natural leader out of the two of us, and a lot more vocal. I tended to be more in the background, making sure that everyone was okay, happy and comfortable one-to-one.

We did the first eight week's session together. I think I'd seen more of Craig than I had seen of anyone else during this time. We were attracting people that were fitter and healthier; we took that as a compliment because it meant our sessions were suitable for more people.

After just four weeks, we had 60 members all paying 99 pounds a month. We were made up with this because we already knew that we were covering our costs of the schools, and the franchise fees and that meant me and Craig were saving a little bit every month before we started paying ourselves. We did the first 12 months without taking a penny from the business so that we could build up a 'buffer' in the accounts.

After eight weeks, we had about 110 members paying 99 pounds a month. That was our target before we started, we had no idea we'd meet it within eight weeks. We wanted to reach 10,000 pounds a month.

It sounds very good when I put it down like this; however, by the end of the eight week, I was tired, stressed out, emotional, fed up, and I had absolutely no life feeling sorry for myself. My only friend was Craig, the only person I spoke to was Craig, the members, and it was all really about work. That was it.

It's funny because people who think that they know me will think that I've always found things relatively easy and taken everything in my stride. However, it was far from that. I've always seemed to have the trouble of not being able to switch off properly. At the end of the day, the thoughts on business, what's happening next, and what's happened doesn't end just because you think you should be sleeping.

I had many sleepless nights when we first set up the business. Tossing and turning, worrying about money, worrying about paying off the credit cards I maxed out to pay for the franchise. I was running on adrenaline most of the time at first. I would struggle to stay awake when I should have been awake, and people were talking to me, or I was out for dinner, or I was watching TV.

Then I'd go to bed and I'd be wide awake, the thoughts, the questions, all rushing through my mind. Night after night. It became very frustrating, and I didn't know how to deal with it or who to talk to about it. There were period of months when I didn't sleep at the start. It was difficult to wake up, flip the switch, and try to be one of these people who had to motivate everyone else around them, feeling absolutely drained myself, but I couldn't just give up, I wasn't just physically on my knees, I was financially too; so it HAD to work.

We're doing sessions 6:00 a.m. until 8:00 a.m. every morning and 5:00 p.m. until 7:30 p.m. every evening. During the day, we were meeting members, potential members, and doing various consultations with them, because they bought full support with their membership. That was draining. I've never felt as tired as I did back then, so that led us to mistake number one. We started to employ people and employ friends. That was a recipe for disaster and something I would never do again.

After we had been running six weeks, things were good and we wanted to continue to build the momentum. So we decided to contact one of the Daily Deal sites to run an offer on Boxing Day, which was about four weeks later; we knew it would be a day that would do well.

We got the deal set up so that people get a month at less than half price to give them a good chance to try us out. In addition, it gave us another way to get our name out there.

We never imagined how busy it was going to get. We sold over 140 people in one day; I remember contacting them to try to end the deal early, but they weren't able to with it being Boxing Day.

Our first session into January, and we had 64 people turn up to the first session. It was absolute chaos. Craig was away in Brazil at the time. I'll never forget when it was about 5:45 a.m., fifteen minutes before the first session started. I was setting up, and there was people just walking in, more and more and more.

I panicked and we ended up having to move to the big hall in the school for that month. We were actually praying at the time that all these people wouldn't carry on when their deal ran out. Luckily, we only signed up about half of them, and people were moving from the busiest sessions to our quieter sessions, as they realised which ones suited them best, both time-wise and how busy it was.

The Friendship Zone

After about 12 weeks, we took on our first number of staff. The first thing we decided to do was take from the sales manager because this meant that Craig and I could focus on the general running of the business and they could deal with sales and membership.

It meant that she would go through all the sales process, which was a real relief for me. I still wasn't 100% comfortable talking to people about money. And still to this day, it's something I get on edge about when I know the topic is coming up. Shortly after we took on the sales manager, who I should mention this time was a good friend of mine, she started to do her own thing.

When she started doing her own thing running her own offers, it all looked and sounded great because we were signing more and more people up, and the business revenue was climbing too. The best intentions were there, however the decisions that were being made were having a big impact on the members. Nevertheless, we realised quite quickly that people talk and people talk about how much they were paying because we were aware that Fit Body wasn't a cheap option.

When the conversations between members started, people wanted to check that they were paying the going rate. Then when it became clear that people were getting cheaper rates based on deals that she had run, this put Craig and I in a very difficult position, constantly being questioned by people who are paying the full price which was £99 a month versus some people who are getting offers because a few of them are joined at once.

Whilst I say that the sales manager started running her own offers and different prices, I should make it clear that it was originally set out to be corporate rates. This is where we would give a discounted rate for a company if they had 10 or more members of staff sign up. And most of the time there would be more than 10 saying they were going to sign up.

However, when it came to the crunch and getting their card details for them to join and ultimately getting them committed, we often found the numbers dwindled and we'd end up with six or seven. And we had the choice to either sign them up or lose them altogether, and she did decide to take them on. It was a decision that she had made, and at the time, really a decision that Craig and I had pretty much left her to make herself. Something that looking back on it really did cause a few issues later on.

This left us with a really tough decision on exactly what to do next. Do we up these other people's prices and run the risk of them leaving? Do we reduce the others, or do we weather the storm and just hope that people start to understand that it was just because a few people that signed up together? At the time, we just decided to leave things as they were and it settled after a while for us, even though it was unneeded pressure at the time.

We were being questioned left, right, and centre, about why some people were paying less than others, and why they got a deal and others didn't. It was very difficult to manage and trying to remove the friendships was hard. It was even more difficult for me to question her and decide on what to do about the whole situation.

After months of Craig and me literally avoiding the hotel we were based at, because it was so awkward being around this, we made the tough decision to terminate her contract.

Something that gave us both many sleepless nights.

However, something we knew we had to do in order to make our business a success. It's safe to say that doing something like this made me realise how tough operating a business was going to get, the tough decisions and the amount of friends that I could possibly lose, or upset, it emotionally wiped me out. We did get advice on this decision before it was made and it was how we learnt that there are people out there to help business owners understand laws, make decisions and ultimately do things in the best way to continue to grow.

After a tough decision of getting rid of the sales manager, and many more sleepless nights, the negativity we received really made me question my job as a business owner, I was just a personal trainer trying to chase the dream. This wasn't in the plan, this wasn't in the photos on Facebook with the wads of cash, nice cars and bling, and this certainly wasn't in my thought process prior to starting up. It was supposed to be easy; it was supposed to be an easy life. How wrong was I?

Stepping Out to Look In

I decided that something needed to change within our business; we needed to operate things slightly different. We took a step out and looked at what things we knew we have to be in control of and what things we could perhaps get other people to do. After the backlash of members talking about different prices and people being unhappy, it became very clear that Craig and I have to be in control of the memberships and sales side of things.

This meant that we decided it was best to take on some personal trainers. We looked for the various different personal trainers and wanted people with experience. However, finding personal trainers with experience was difficult, particularly as we were a new business. That led us to go up to the boxing gym where we knew there were quite a few young, hungry personal trainers up there looking for a chance in the fitness industry.

In a short space of time, we took on three personal trainers who were great. We had a really good team at the start and things really started to fall into place with our business. We were growing our team, we were growing our brand, and the money started to come in more and more every month.

I have to say it was probably one of the happiest times of my life. I even started to have a little bit of a personal life again and that's where I met the most beautiful woman in the world when she joined Fit Body, Elly Le Cornu She asked me on a date after a few months of being at boot camp and after debating if it was unprofessional or not, I said yes. It's safe to say I've never looked back from that time.

After Elly had been a member for a few months, I started to get asked a few questions by her about nutrition and about training, and she came in to see me for a consultation where we discussed her diet. At the time, I thought she was just a general client that needed more information, ultimately wanting to improve her own health and fitness.

Then, she started texting me asking me a few more questions and I responded. I never in a million years thought that she would be interested in me, until we started to talk more and more, and it almost seemed we were talking constantly from the moment of waking up to going to bed via text. Eventually, she had the lady balls to ask me out on a date and I was shaking with excitement and of course I said yes.

When we went on our first date, we spoke about if I would have ever asked her out and I probably wouldn't have had the bottle. Partly because she was way out of my league, and because I wouldn't step over the mark with a member. I asked her to suggest a place and she suggested sushi because knowing I'm a personal trainer, she thought I'd like to eat healthy. Little did she know that it was my worst nightmare. However, I agreed to go and actually didn't find the food too bad.

The company was much better though and we had a great night. This was the start of the great relationship that was going to form almost overnight for us. I think we both knew that we were meant to be from that first date. We got to know each other day by day and spent every minute we could together.

When Elly and I first started dating, I was in the build up to my final boxing fight, so I was always trying to watch my weight. Usually when I tried to lose the weight I would often not eat for days.

However, meeting Elly every night for dinner meant that I ate healthy, well-balanced meal every evening. At the time, it was just an excuse to see Elly. I think we used our love of food and training to build a strong relationship together. We used to go out running in the evenings and then go home and eat. I'd cook one night, Elly would cook the next.

We'd always take Alfie, the dog, out for a walk as well. Alfie was Elly's dog back then, but now he's ours. Looking back at it from here, I can clearly see how much I was on the go at that time.

I was getting up at4:00 a.m.in the morning to start work, working all day until late in the evening, and then still having to train on top of that, as well as trying to watch my diet and keep my energy levels high. It was a very tough time at the start of the business; things were coming from all angles.

After we'd been operating for about seven months, Craig and I went on a Mastermind to San Diego. It was with the Fit Body Boot Camp franchise. At the time, we were still in two minds about whether the mastermind or even franchise was the right thing for us or not. It put us in good stead to start the business and build up quickly. However, we knew we wanted to start at more locations.

We were thinking of what we had faced with having triple the outgoings concerning franchise fees. Then when we got to the three-day-long event, we spent the whole of the first day talking about a system, which wasn't really related to the Franchise and what we needed. It didn't really help our business.

Craig and I were left frustrated; we really didn't know what to do. The following day, the same kind of thing happened again; I think us being British and everyone else being American didn't overly help. This rather reassured us that being in the Mastermind wasn't the right thing for us.

We had invested over £2,000 on the flights and a hotel while we were over there. However, we did manage to get a good few night outs, which was really good. Craig and I loved going to the states to see all these American cities and have great nights out, even if that wasn't the purpose of the trip.

Soon after this trip to San Diego, Fit Body grew from 1 location to 4 boot camp locations and 5 trainers within the next 6 months. In addition, we had some epic news that Elly was pregnant too, something we had discussed but couldn't believe how quickly it happened and EVERYTHING was falling into place.

Growing Too Fast

As the business was growing from strength to strength, and we opened more locations, I soon started to realise that we had possibly made another mistake.

After running our Fit Body Boot camp at one location for about eight months, we were under quite a bit of pressure to run more and more locations, was it a compliment? It's worth pointing out in Jersey that it takes no more than 20 minutes to drive anywhere in the mornings when we ran our busiest sessions. Yet the pressure from people living the other side of the island (no more than 5 miles away) to open a location up there for them, was overwhelming and so we thought long and hard about it because we didn't want to rush it, but I guess we thought with our ego and the thought of running more locations made us look good. However, there seemed to be a demand there for it, and we had all the staff that we needed to do so.

***So, this is what has led us to open location number two. After that, we very quickly decided to open three new locations within the space of about five months. Thus, we went from a business with one boot camp location to four, almost overnight. This stretched our business. Consequently, Craig and I had to work even more hours. And I have to be honest; we didn't see our income multiply by four when we opened four times as many locations. In retrospect, we would have been better with sticking with one location, and possibly, at best open one more location and take things slower.

This also made it much more of a challenge, covering holidays, managing staff, paying bills on 4 locations the whole lot was frustrating however the business still continued to grow, and our profit was still going up month on month.

However, looking back at it now, it wasn't really a good return of investment. We were investing a lot more time and effort into the business, and getting more and more grief from people, or more and more demands off people for very little more in return. In fact, I became more of a business manager than a coach, when coaching was my passion. This became very frustrating very quickly, and soon I was fed up and was not enjoying my job at all.

In addition, whenever I went to one of the locations, the other location would moan that I hadn't been to that one for a while. Unfortunately, I'm very good, but I could never split myself into four. This made me resent delivering the boot camp sessions because I knew the hassle it would cause.

Now I look at things as a return of investment (ROI) and that's an investment of both time, effort and money, so if doing loads of more work, loads more pressure, and more stress for just a small amount of more money, then it's really not a worthwhile investment, I wouldn't go near it.

You could say we expanded based on our ego rather than our business minds.

I'll never forget when we had been running Fit Body about a year, I had a rare night out on the town, and I had a couple of drunk friends telling me how I'd made it. Sounded great to hear it from a friend, but this wasn't what my ego needed.

I was doing really well, and inside of me I was really just thinking, I was one of those people who I followed and was painting the ideal lifestyle all over social media for all to see, which probably gave them the thought that I had made it easy.

However, this wasn't the case, as we all now know, I was working long hours and really wasn't enjoying life at the time. The only thing I had going for me was that Elly and I had the strong relationship and we were expecting our child. This was the one thing that kept me going all the way through this, I was questioning if the work was really worth it. However, the fact that I was going to be a dad and I was with the woman of my dreams kept me going.

When we had Fit Body, particularly early on, we had numerous parties for birthdays and for Christmas. We always spent a small fortune on food, drink and prizes. It was something that I thought we were doing as an investment. Because though it was nice, it did need to benefit us at the same time. However, what we did find was people were bringing old members, and it was almost taken advantage of.

I learned quite early of the real need to set boundaries in places to make sure that things don't get out of control, and to make sure that generosity isn't taken for granted, because although the money wasn't physically out of my pocket, the more we spent the less we paid ourselves. Frustrating.

On one party, we even had former members that hadn't stayed with us because they'd gone to somebody else turn up and take a free drink and food. At the time, I stayed calm and just didn't let them know it bothered me. However, you do realise that loyalty isn't a quality everyone possesses, even if they'll pop in to gate crash a party for a free drink and food.

We had spent a lot of time and effort on these members. They left us, which was no problem at all, but then to come to our parties really left me with severe frustration, which made me to consider not running any more of the parties, as it was something that drained a lot of time and energy from me during the process of trying to organise everything.

In fact, I'll never forget our first Birthday party; we spent over £4k and we had over 120 people attend, it was a great night, but yet again it was more of an ego based decision to have a party like this rather than a business based one.

I think coming to terms with the fact that you have to put a business hat on to operate a business is a big pill to swallow as often it means looking at the bigger picture and asking how the business will benefit from this.

Leaving the Franchise

After we opened three new locations of Fit Body Boot Camp Jersey, we were faced with a tough decision. We either had to pay 4 times more franchise fees for the exactly the same service or leave the franchise. This led Craig and I to remodel our business slightly and operate it under our own terms. A tough decision we didn't take lightly, but we found it a positive thing in the long run because we knew we could adapt and improvise things how we wanted, and it meant that in the future, if we wanted to sell it would be a much easier process.

When we left the franchise, we dropped the Boot Camp and called it Fit Body Jersey. We re-branded it and started to operate things a bit different to the way that they do in the franchise. We started to target different muscle groups every day, and made things a little bit structured around our clients' goals, because after all, we have to start to attract people who are fitter, as well as those looking to lose weight. This was something that was seen as a positive by both the members and the staff too.

Although it was a tough decision to leave the franchise because it did help us to build a business more or less overnight, it was certainly a good thing in the long run. Looking back at it now, although I do miss the trips to the states for it.

After leaving the franchise, we got a business coach/mentor Paul Mort, who's a UK based coach and somebody we felt was the right person to help bring our business forward.

One thing we learned very quickly was that we've been putting on an image to attract more people more than being our ourselves to attract the right people. Thus, we began to be more ourselves and started to realise that the people we didn't really click as well with started to leave, but that then opened the door to people we actually clicked with and got along well with.

It's safe to say that over the next few months we saw a big swing in the type of clients we were attracting and kept. We started to see more and more people that were just like us personality wise. More and more people we would be happy to go out for a drink with or spend time with voluntarily as well as for our work.

As soon as I started being true to myself, I just used my own personality all the time and found that 'my type' of people would approach me and things became a lot less draining. I couldn't believe it just by being myself; I found that I was attracting the types of people I really got on well with.

Rather than putting on this act, which I thought I had to, in order to create an image I started to be myself. Also, the energy vampires that seem to suck the life out of me were slowly whittling away. I began to enjoy my job again, even with the long hours it was worth it at the time as I was working with people I really got on well with and liked. This is probably the biggest shift of mindset that I had. It was only just after a few weeks of working with Paul Mort that I established this.

After we had been running for about 18 months, we decided that we would no longer run any big promotions, or any daily deals to get people into our Boot camps because we started to realise that it was taking up a lot of our time and resources and it also wasn't fair on full paying members.

I would get people emailing, when are we running our next promotion, at the time it would annoy me, I wouldn't dream of asking someone when they're next going to run an offer.

So, we just stopped with the daily deal offers and just offered a week free trial. This meant that people, when they tried us, they were given a week to get to grips with the programme. If it wasn't for them, then that was great. They haven't lost anything, only their time.

For us it meant we had only lost one slot of 15 minutes where we met potential clients for a consultation, discussed their goals, etc. This seemed to run a lot better for us than trying to run big deals to get hundreds and hundreds of people through the door because reality was, we didn't have space for all these people.

Setting Up the Rock

While Fit Body Jersey was bouncing and getting busier and busier, it was great and people started to talk. There was a couple of companies in Jersey doing white collar boxing and it was getting popular, and because Craig and I both had a boxing background, we were approached by many people about us running one, something we previously didn't want to do, it meant much more work, time, and ultimately would take us away from Fit Body.

However, after numerous enquiries we thought we'd be mad not to jump on the opportunity, so we needed to find a base to run this. We found a 'dry storage unit' at the opposite end of town that had been empty for years, it was perfect, had exposed brick, beams and real character to it.

That's where we ended up setting up the Rock Boxing and Fitness Studio, which has a small boxing based gym upstairs, then we had a regular gym downstairs with changing rooms and showers. That was the base for our white-collar events.

Probably the best thing we did with the rock was set it up where it was key fob access. This meant that all members got their own key, and it was completely self-servicing. The beauty behind this meant that we didn't need to manage it, and we didn't need to be there to open or close it up. Yes, we had to invest a little bit more money in getting the right system in place to get the key fob working, slightly higher insurance and a must was having good quality CCTV installed.

However, once that was all done, the cost was pretty much out of the way and going forward, the costs would be minimal, and it means that the gym completely runs itself, and it also means that we don't have to reduce opening hours based on holidays, etc. This made life so much easier and enjoyable because I know that relying on staffing isn't the way I wanted to operate. Looking at it, if I set up a business ever again that was going to involve face-to-face contact, it would be something like this, that is completely self-servicing and I can more or less come and go as I please.

When setting up the Rock Boxing and Fitness studio, we thought it would be a lot easier than it was. Trying to get planning permission to change it from a warehouse into a gym proved more difficult that we imagined it would be. The cost to put in the planning application, application fee, architects fees, then we got the issue that it would be approved provided we put a lift in.

The lift would have costs us about £80,000. To put a little picture in your mind, we have a boxing gym upstairs where there are just boxing bags and a ring with a few dumbbells. Downstairs, we have a fitness studio, which has got loads of normal gym equipment and changing rooms. However, anything you could do upstairs, you could also do downstairs and we had to prove it.

We had to get the architect that managed our application to fight our case. Of course, an architect costs a lot of money, which meant that bills would sharply increase and there would be letters and emails back and forth, which took time. Every e-mail took two or three days to get a reply.

This delayed us by weeks and weeks on our project. It also meant that the gym was getting opened later than we had hoped, and obviously that also had a knock on effect on us starting the business we had spent a lot of time and money working towards. Frustration was at the forefront and it felt and still feels like the authorities don't want new businesses to get up and running without incurring delays and astronomical fees. It also delayed the start of our white-collar boxing training because of all of these fine print things that needed to be amended.

The white-collar boxing comprises of having a 12-week training program where people who never boxed before learned how to box. This meant working more hours in the evenings and during Sunday mornings as well, which meant our weekends were non-existent. However, the reason we decided to do this is that we see it as another opportunity to set up another company and target a different niche.

We kept this completely separate to Fit Body because we felt it was targeting different people, and we always thought it would be our little place in the future, I remember a quote from our business coach at the time, Paul Mort, most of the time in business you finish it with one of two things:

1- You go bust.
2- You sell it.

Therefore, we knew that if we ever wanted to sell Fit Body, we would still have the rock- one thing we did which was a stroke of genius.

When we finally decided that we were definitely going to run our first white-collar, Craig managed to contact one of his old friends from Liverpool to secure Derry Matthews to come and judge the event. He was our guest of honour.

He refereed the 10 fights and it was great for us and the Boxers to meet a world champion. He was at the weigh-in as well with his belt. The whole experience for us, the boxers, and the people, who came to watch, was overwhelming.

We raised over £20,000 on that event and it's something that I'm extremely proud of. All the hard work did pay off and what 's more, although it was working a bit longer hours, it was relatively stress free because we had someone organise the event for us (the art of delegating things).

As the business was growing, it's clear now that at the time, that the only thing I was worried about was the business. Ask me anything about the business and I knew the answer. How many clients we had signed up in the last week, month, two months, even three months. Ask me how many clients we had lost. Ask me any expenses we had done. I knew the answers.

Then ask me anything else that was going on in the real world, I didn't have a clue. I didn't know what was going on with my family. I didn't know what was going on with my friends. I didn't know what was going on in the news. I'd say, I was living in my own little bubble, forgetting everyone else around me, including Elly to a large degree too.

I'm not really sure when I started to realise that this was happening, or what triggered the realisation but I'm glad I did. And I turned it off when I wasn't working and started to listen to people more. I stopped talking, silence. Tried to stop thinking about the business and myself, and put more focus on people around me. This was the best thing I ever did because it gave me a little bit more mental clearance and helped build my relationships.

Bouncing at Fit Body

As we kept growing more and more, month per month, we decided we need to give somebody a little bit more responsibility, so it meant Craig and I had more time to continue focussing on the things our business coach had us working on to keep growing the business and looking after the members.

That was when we made my friend the head trainer, and the mistake of employing a friend haunted me yet again. We showed him everything we knew, from advertising, marketing, systems, how to get clients, build membership bases; everything, literally inside out.

I even had so much time for him that when his parents threw him out of his house, I let him stay at my flat for a couple of months, and I moved in with Elly.

Whilst I was working these long hours, probably about 14 hours a day, five and sometimes six days a week and a few hours on a Sunday too. Particularly at the start. I was still spending time painting this perfect lifestyle, this perfect picture for people to see. It's safe to say that I was leading with my ego. I was letting people think that I was loving life.

However, inside it was a different story completely and at the time, not many people knew it. I was tired, run down, fed up, and I'd lost all my social ties. I soon started to realise that I was doing what probably most of these people I had seen put in the pictures of the wads of cash, and the fancy cars were doing.

Something I now know is that I was seeking other people's approval, rather than just living my life the way that I wanted to do and being honest, I had the income to do that, but I guess I kept striving for more, through ambition and greed. I was looking for constant validation from people that, I didn't really know, let alone have time to like.

My Life Would Never be the Same Again

Shortly after Elly and I got together, we knew it was for real 100% that we were going to be together forever and we discussed our future and how much we wanted a family. Elly has PCOS (Polycystic Ovary Syndrome), which she thought may hinder her chances of getting pregnant, so we decided to start trying but were relaxed about it; if it happened, it happened.

Month 1 of this 'relaxed approach', Elly got pregnant, so happy and excited, but we also couldn't believe how quickly it had happened.

When Elly was about 7 months pregnant, I decided to go out for a little drive with Craig, and then ended up coming home with a Range Rover. I remember sending a picture to Elly and telling her this is our new car, I'm surprised she didn't go into early labour. The truth was, we didn't need a new car and we had two perfectly working cars with a baby around the corner, it probably wasn't the wisest choice to make.

However, now I can say that I bought this based on my ego. I bought this thinking about what other people would think, and what other people would perceive when I had this car. I was made up. The people I had telling me that they were jealous of the car. The people that were telling me they couldn't believe I had this car, and it was their dream car, and I had it. I was made up, 25 years old, and I was driving around in my dream car already. I was telling myself I'd made it. The ego couldn't have gotten much bigger at that time.

Elly's pregnancy was a relatively straightforward one up until 32 weeks. Then, unfortunately, her health took a turn for the worse. She couldn't eat anything and was crippled by an illness she had in the past that was flaring back up (sphincter of oddi dysfunction), because her body was under more pressure, her organs are under strain and she couldn't do anything. So, from 32 weeks on, we were going to the hospital every week.

There was another issue. I had a business trip planned to Portugal when Elly was 35 weeks pregnant and I couldn't pull out of it or, should I say, I decided I couldn't pull out of it at the time. I'll never forget getting a flight to London.

I had to then, before I got my connecting flight to Portugal, I called Elly to make sure that the check-up went okay. Looking at it now, I left my sick girlfriend, heavily pregnant to go on a business trip to learn more, I seriously have no idea what I was thinking at the time.

Something that really ate me up inside at the time, but for some reason, I chose my business over being there to help Elly. I really don't know how I would have coped if I had missed the birth.

I got back from the course absolutely fine, and at 37 weeks they decided to induce Elly more to put an end to her agony. She had an 18-hour labour and I was there throughout her labour, I say that I was there but I was actually on my phone, replying to e-mails, managing staff, contacting clients, etc. Again, something that really eats me up inside, because I was choosing work, again, over family.

Then, beautiful little Aoife-Mae was born by emergency C-section. I had to go to work the next day, I did reduce my working hours for about a week, but didn't take a single day off. Again, something that I'm ashamed of, because I chose chasing work, chasing money over my girlfriend and daughter at the time.

Becoming a dad was the best gift I've ever been given. It's safe to say that when Aoife-Mae was first born, my head wasn't in the right place for me to do what dads should do. I'm ashamed to say that I didn't really prioritise things as I should have done.

Elly and Aoife-Mae ended up having to take back seats; often coming after business. This is something that I'm extremely embarrassed thinking about it right now. However, I guess it paid the bills, and that's what I was telling myself at the time, that one day it would get better.

If I were to go back and repeat my time now, I would definitely have sold the business much earlier, as soon as I knew that I would be able to want to spend more time at home. The truth was, before Aoife-Mae was born, I didn't have the slightest idea of how I would feel about becoming a dad, and my thought process changed overnight.

When Aoife-Mae was born, I made out a serious priority shift. I made Aoife-Mae and Elly my priority; they were definitely the two most important things in my life. The reality was they were, but unfortunately, the choices I made, the actions I took, sometimes created a very different picture.

From trying to earn more to feed the ego, and get the things like fancy cars, smart clothes and the wads of cash, to earning more to provide a good life for Elly and Aoife-

Mae so that they're proud of me; something I never thought I'd feel like.

Then again, looking back at this time makes me so fortunate that Elly was so understanding throughout.

I was constantly putting work before them, making decisions that meant I'd spend more time away from them just to run the business, just to keep things going and keep driving things forward. Working early mornings, evenings, missing bath times and bed times ate me up inside. All because I was chasing that "wad of cash" or another holiday. I'm still not sure whether this was led by guilt, greed, or stupidity, however, looking back at it now, if I had the chance to make these decisions again, never in a million years would I chose to work or my business over Elly and Aoife-Mae.

Just a few months after Aoife-Mae was born, it was Elly's birthday. I decided that I would surprise her. I didn't tell her what we were doing. I booked a hotel at Longueville Manor. It's one of the nicest hotels in Jersey, and decided that I was going to pop the question.

I never forget the day when I went up to ask her dad if I could ask her to marry me. Shaking like a leaf, I couldn't even get out of the car before I'd asked him. He came up to the window of the door, and I asked him, and he said yes straight away. Now the hardest questions following that had to be to ask Elly. We got into the hotel room, I couldn't wait till dinner like I had mapped out in my head, was shitting it too much. I got down on to my knees, and I asked her the question. I think I was crying as I asked her, and she said yes straight away. This made me be the happiest bloke alive.

Whilst Elly was pregnant, we discussed the various options about her -- whether she was going to go back to work in the finance industry, not work at all, or do something else. She was not overly enjoying her career in finance, so we decided that she should qualify as a personal trainer, and fulfil her passion of helping others.

She studied sports psychology at university, and always wanted to help people in a health and fitness environment, but has never been in a position to do it. Therefore, almost overnight, she started studying. Every spare moment she had she was studying before she went to work, after she got home, and then, once Aoife-Mae was born, she continued to study. This was the first time I've ever really seen someone working so hard towards something that she really wanted, and I admired that.

That was a lesson that I wanted to remember, that when you really want something, you have to work for it because it wasn't easy. At the time Aoife-Mae had her nap, she spent time studying, learning new things, and picking up new tricks. She had also spent as much time as she could trying to get to the gym to learn more, working it around my working hours or our parents helping us out; we were fortunate to have such good supporting families because they were really helpful for us and always willing to look after Aoife-Mae if it meant Elly could do a bit more on her course.

I think, when Elly qualified, I was more excited and ecstatic than she was. I was literally over the moon. My best friend and fiancée had fulfilled her dream and had become a personal trainer. I was so, so happy and proud, we didn't tell people while she was studying either so it was so hard to keep it a secret, as I wanted the world to know.

I knew we'd be going to work together and doing things to help each other and our clients. However, I never imagined what was going to happen further down the line if we go into business together.

I guess you could say her qualifying boosted my passion and motivation to keep helping more people every day, and that's something I'm really grateful for. As soon as Elly qualified, she did get busy pretty much overnight because she had been somebody who practiced what she preached.

She was training during her pregnancy, which made her receive some negativity but she kept going and stayed in good shape and started training pretty much straight away after giving birth. That's where I started to realise the attraction for people practicing what they preach and how much it attracts clients, even if it does have some people perceiving it as a negative thing. I was living off the name I had built at Fit Body rather than practicing what I preach.

Trip to Liverpool I'll Never Forget

For the last four or five years, I've always been to the dentist in Liverpool, since I got my veneers done. Aoife-Mae was about four weeks old, we decided to go away for a few days to Liverpool to see my dentist, do a bit of shopping, and have a little bit of a rest with her. It's safe to say that the trip was far from restful. But Aoife-Mae was sleeping really well, however, during the five mornings we were there. I had three early morning wake-ups from members who were waiting outside at the various locations because staff had slept in.

As a result of that, we had numerous cancellations in a short period of time. People being fed up, and it really frustrated me; to be honest, I would do the same if I got up at 5 a.m. to work out and paying £100 a month for the trainer not to show up. I really didn't know what to do, but when I got back I had to apologise to the members, and then try to put a system in place where it was a little bit easier to make sure that all the staff woke up in time. This resulted in me or one of the staff calling everyone, and that increased my workload.

Unfortunately, I soon started to realise that you can't always guarantee that the person's going to get up. I have to admit, it happened to me once. I slept in, and ever since then I've always set two alarms, one on my phone, another on Elly's phone. Mine only goes on snooze about five times before I get out of bed. However, I still don't allow the same thing to happen more than once.

This soon became very frustrating for me over the short period of time; people not getting up and it ALWAYS came back on me, the shitty phone calls, and the shitty emails.

For a month or two, we very rarely got a week where somebody didn't sleep in. I always appreciated that it was early, however these people were paid well to do a job, and all they have to do is turn up on time, make sure the equipment was ready, and train the people to a good standard.

At this time I was ready to just shut the business down, because whether its right or not, I care about what people think of me, and at the time they probably weren't thinking good things about me because I was the one being vented to. I was the one picking up the shit, and I guess rightly so, it was my business but that doesn't make it any easier to swallow.

The Departure of a good friend

Just a short time after making my good friend head trainer, he left us because he decided that he wanted to go and work with children with special needs. However, the night of his last day with us, I realised that he had 'un-friended' me on Facebook and announced he was launching his own business. Sounds kind of pathetic now but I was literally gutted he had un-friended me.

He copied pretty much everything we had done, and everything we were doing. It left me feeling extremely upset, disappointed, angry, and questioning if I should trust anyone. It's safe to say that I had many more sleepless nights thinking, tossing and turning about what had happened. Was it my fault? Had I done something wrong? Had I shown him too much?

All these questions were running through my head day after day. I became very, very angry about it all.

Not too long after this happened and he set up his own business, I started to get more and more people come up to me, telling me about the things that he'd copied me on.

I was shown video after video, Facebook post after Facebook post that he had done and even spoke like me, copied text that I've used, and at the time, I was frustrated. I was frustrated because I think people thought that it was the true him.

However, now I can laugh about it because those people that know me and those people that have gotten to know me have realised and seen how we differ and the experience I have. The frustrations that I once had have now gone.

They've turned into laughter because I now know that I've been true to myself all the way through it. Although, at the time, I had good family support. They helped me get through the tough times and deal with the frustration without losing my patience or temper.

I am just thankful that my business or more so my income was not really affected too much by this, even though I was personally affected because I have to be honest, I was really hurt. I was upset. I was frustrated, and ultimately had just lost someone who I looked to like a little brother. A big lesson for me was not to give someone too much when it comes to business, and I'm thankful I learnt this earlier on.

Knowing that someone can copy what you do but he or she will never be you is a comforting thought when in this kind of situation. He does his own thing and I do mine.

Even though he left on bad terms and bad things have been said over the 18 months, since then I now know it really was just because he wanted the best for himself and his future even though it did hurt when he left. I guess you could say I wore my heart on my sleeve and it got hurt. A lesson I've learnt from, and I won't be making that mistake again of employing good friends.

Now, I do generally wish him all the very best because he is a hard working bloke who wants the best for himself and his family just like I do. It's just a shame that we did part on such bad terms, because we both do have a lot of similarities. We're both business-minded, very driven, and only want the best for our family and ourselves.

The Welsh Wizard came to us

Shortly after he left and set upon his own, we received numerous applications for jobs. I think people knew that we would be looking for a new trainer.

We got one application from somebody who has previously sent us a form, Dean Price, he was persistent but from Wales so I didn't know much about him. But I decided to meet him for a chat. I knew very little about him so I already had a negative thought in my mind before I even met him.

However, he rocked up 45 minutes earlier for his interview dressed in a suit. It was a first for me. I'd never met a personal trainer who turned up to an interview in a suit. However, we clicked straightaway. There was something about this guy -- he was really passionate, energetic and ultimately the type of person that I felt I was just before we set up Fit Body.

He was so passionate about helping people and about trying to help Fit Body to continue to grow and stay the best boot camp in Jersey. Therefore, we offered him the job, as a Personal Trainer at the Rock and coach for Fit Body helping us to look after clients, a bit more TLC and he was great at it. Within a very short period, he got the team absolutely bouncing again. Everybody was feeling positive.

Things were really good all-around within the business; in fact I sort of started to enjoy managing it again, he had a great personality and got on well with all the members. The feedback we had about him was brilliant. The funny thing was, when he came to shadow us for some other sessions he was silent; didn't say a word. Then, when he delivered the sessions, he came into his own and you couldn't shut him up.

Over the next 10 months, we started to develop a good working relationship, but more so a great friendship with each other and as a whole team. I latched onto Dean really well and we became very good friends, someone I trusted, and someone I got on well with.

When Dean and I started to get to become better friends, I started to really get my passion back for helping people. I started to realise that running the business or operating a company managing staff was not for me.

I started to realise that I didn't want staff, I didn't want to manage people, I wanted to coach people who needed and wanted help. This quickly became very clear for me. And I started to look at ways that I could start to be more involved in coaching people and less involved in operating the business.

Therefore, over the next few months, I started training personally a few more clients to help utilise that passion and help me feel like I was doing more than just managing a business. It's funny, looking back at it now, five years ago; all I wanted to do was own a business.

I wanted to be the top dog. I had the dream of sitting in the office while business went on. I now realised that I wanted that for my ego, not for my passion. And I found myself almost swapping my passion for money, now I'm in a position where delivering my passion is the only goal I have.

If I can make good money from it, then I'm really happy. I guess what you could say back then before starting out the business; I had shiny objects syndrome. I was chasing money. I guess a way to look at it was the more clients I had the more stuff I could buy that I didn't really need. Wanting to earn more and more and more and at 25 years old, taking in a six figure salary was great. I was really happy, had a nice car, it paid for our dream wedding but it didn't satisfy me.

I was getting home each day fed up, stressed out, and annoyed with it all. I had lost some 'good friends' who weren't interested when they saw the success come, and I had started to become quite secluded from everyone. The only thing I had was Aoife-Mae and Elly, they were the ones, the only things that kept me going. They were the ones that drove me to go to work every day, otherwise I probably would have packed it in a long time ago.

Up to this time, we were still operation at the Radisson Hotel where the gym was in all honesty too small for us, not to mention staffing it was a pain. Whilst we were still there, things were a little bit uncomfortable. We were working in the corridor, which was pretty much in the way of guests, staff and anyone trying to use the facility. So when we were sitting at the computer, trying to do administrative work, we were having people coming up to us, asking us questions, general enquiries, either about the business or about the hotel gym. It could even just be staff wanting to have a conversation with us about things not work related too. This made it extremely challenging to stay in the actual workplace to do our work.

Both Craig and I decided to start doing more work from home because there were fewer distractions. Therefore, I started spending more time at my laptop or my phone getting work done; however, by me not being physically at work, I think people thought that I was being lazy. People didn't see the work that was going on behind the scenes. They thought I was just there for the sessions and went home and did nothing all day. They didn't see the e-mails flying, they didn't see the calls, they didn't see the texts I was responding to, and they didn't see the administration that I had to do behind the business to get it busier.

This became very frustrating when I had jokes, or digs from people about how little I was actually present at the work place. I think that sometimes the staff didn't appreciate the amount of admin we had to do behind the scenes to keep the business running and working well. Truth be told, if they would have done the admin and I could have gone back to training people, I'd have bitten their hand off to do it.

Not being actually present possibly led to some of them not staying with us quite as long as they could have done if we were there more. It was frustrating because I would have had that same thought six months before. If I didn't see someone at work, I just assumed that they probably weren't doing anything. If they weren't training people, what else was there to do? However, this fast learning curve I soon started to realise the work that was involved in getting stuff done, holding the business up, continuing to help it grow forwards.

Our First Family Holiday

Later that summer, Elly and I took Aoife-Mae to Ireland to see my Nan for her 75th birthday. All of my family was there so it was good for them to meet Aoife-Mae for the first time. We then went on to Marbella for two weeks after that, so ended up being just over 3 weeks off work; the longest time I'd taken away from the business since being self-employed. It was an exciting prospect to have that time off but also knowing I was away for almost a month and with how fast the business was moving I was a little scared too.

During the trip to Marbella and Ireland, I made the choice not to read any e-mails, open my inbox at all, for nearly four weeks. It was something I found hard mentally, but I did it.

However, there was a downside to this. I got back from my holiday and had thousands of e-mails, literally. I had put an Out Of Office reply on, for urgent things to be addressed to Craig but still had people e-mailing me, chasing me up, did you get my e-mail I sent, did you get that e-mail. I came back and within a week was more stressed out than I was before I went away.

That holiday seemed a distant memory and it took five or six day's solid email reading to get through that inbox. Even then, I have to admit I ended up just deleting quite a few e-mails and not bothering to read them because I really didn't feel like I had the time or energy to start chasing through all those e-mails. I thought if it was important, they would get back in touch with me and then I'd be able to deal with it then.

I learned the lesson quite quickly that sometimes spending an hour or two a day, even whilst I'm on holiday, can really ease the pressure and stress for when I get back from holiday.

Everything was good at the business when I left it; however, as we were getting busier and busier, it had started to create a few problems in the hotel that we were working from at the time. I think the hotel expected us to operate without running a business; they just wanted us to man the hotel gym. Complaint after complaint rolled in from the hotel residents that the gym was too busy.

Yes, it was busy with our staff working, training clients, and we ran boot camps there. It started to put a mental pressure on Craig and I to find somewhere else to relocate our business for us, the staff, and the clients.

When we knew we needed to find a bigger place to run our business, because the hotel was far too small for us to expand any further, we spent loads of time and effort going to see different venues or different places that we could rent. We were getting advice on what to do, and basically trying to make sure we didn't make any mistakes here.

The difficult part was that we knew we were going to have to get planning consent to operate as a fitness studio or a health clinic, or basically run along them sort of lines. This process can take years at times.

Getting planning consent for anything fitness related is something that in Jersey seemed to be very difficult, even though you're going to be employing local staff and giving young school leavers a job in something they enjoy too.

This left us frustrated, and trying to secure a long enough lease to make the money worth its while was proving difficult. We went to see one place that had potential, but we could only get a three-year lease on it, which meant by the time we'd invested in equipment and the building, we would struggle to see a return in investment. This led us to find Castle Quay, which location-wise was perfect, just the rent was much higher than anywhere else, and they weren't budging on that or the 12 year lease they wanted.

The Mindset Course

Even though business was booming, I was still quite angry with my 'friend' setting up a replica business to mine even though everything else in my life was going really well.

I was happily engaged.

Had a beautiful daughter.

Business was booming.

I still had part of me eaten up until I went on a course with Paul Mort; he knew of my frustrations and thought it would be good for me.

This course was different from any other I had been on, it was more about mindset, and I began to question things in my head, then realised that a lot of the stories I was telling myself weren't true.

When we signed up for this mindset course, it was something I was a little anxious about because I've always been somebody who puts a barrier up before being in touch with my emotions. I think that my time in the army made me want to hide my feelings, living with 40 other blokes and showing your sensitive side doesn't go down well.

I used to try not to let people know what's on my mind or how I feel, partly through embarrassment, partly through pride and possibly my ego being dented, as well. So I went on this course, and it was uncomfortable, in fact very uncomfortable. I had to sit in front of the other seven or eight people that were on the course and tell them about my deepest and darkest thoughts, the thoughts that ate me up inside.

I used my friend that had left the company and set up his own thing, copying what I had done as an example of something that had annoyed me. Then doing this course and the work that we did in front of everybody turned it around, and I realised that all the problems or the issues were in my head, and I was allowing that. I soon saw that the only way I could relieve myself of those frustrations was by questioning my thoughts. So that straightaway changed my whole mindset, and my whole thought process about the way I would run the rest of my life.

That course, I have to say, in three days, completely transformed my life and the way I felt and still feel about things. The problem was his, not mine. I carried on with my business, and things continued to grow.

I started to win battles in my head again and realising that, things were better than I actually thought they were.

After returning from the course with Paul, I decided that a few things needed to change. He'd give us a book called, *Loving What Is* by Byron Katie, and we had an option to join for a 90-day life accountability program with him.

We had to look at all the different areas of our lives. Something, I have to be honest, I'd previously never done. I'd always just focused on work, work, work, and forgotten about other things like my relationships (even though Elly was holding me up at the time) and my body (I had let myself go, was an out of shape trainer I used to criticise).

I was a personal trainer, telling people to get in shape. But since I started my business, and Aoife-Mae was born truth be told, I'd become well out of shape. I was very unhappy with my own body shape. He set us a 90-day goal to improve all these areas of our lives.

It just so happened that the 90 days led me up until Elly and I got married. Motivation was on. I booked a photo shoot, and decided to work on all these different areas. For the first time in my life, business never came first. I focused on my relationships; I focused on my body shape, and almost completely ignored the business side of things.

We ended up being kicked out of this course because Craig and I didn't comprise to what we were being set. However, I learned a lot from this. I stopped all the one-way relationships in my life, and soon started to realise that many of the people I thought were my friends weren't quite as interested as they first appeared when I stopped giving.

However, Elly and I got closer and closer, as we planned our wedding in depth together and Aoife-Mae was my best friend; we built the best father daughter relationship I could have imagined.

My priorities were completely different to the way they were just a few weeks before. My trust issues with friends were still there. I didn't really trust anybody that wasn't family. In fact, the only people at this time in my life that I could trust were close family, a few very close friends, (Michael and Katie) and Craig. Craig has been beside me all the way through this, and we've been through some tough times and made some tough decisions together, which meant I knew that I could trust him. We've still never had a crossed word so to speak to this day.

When Elly and I was planning our wedding, we really didn't give any thought to the budget. We just went for it and got exactly what we wanted. We didn't cut any corners whatsoever, it was our day, why should we. We had the money, I have to say, and this is the first time in my life I've ever really acted on what I want without giving a second thought to how much it cost at the time.

We've worked hard and we had enough money saved to have that dream wedding. We had a choice, for us an easy choice. We could either have our dream wedding or use it as a deposit for a house, and I know I would choose our dream wedding every day of the week.

During the 90-day goal, we were also moving location away from the Hotel, because we had outgrown our stay. We were operating out of a tiny little gym with four personal trainers. It was just too small. We decided that we need somewhere bigger and that we didn't have to staff it until9:00 p.m., seven days a week.

Shortly after the Mindset course with Paul, Elly and I took Aoife-Mae to Turkey for a two-week holiday. During this time, I was posting up videos on Facebook as part of the program I decided to join moving forward.

We had to put up videos every day to try to increase our positivity, something I had always, and still struggle to do. Upon doing this, I received a lot of positive feedback. However, I did get some negativity and people basically taking the piss out of me. This was something that I find hard to deal with, but didn't let these people know.

This was probably the first time I'd ever come across some sort of public negativity from doing well. I felt embarrassed and upset at the time. However, when I spoke to Paul about this, the first thing he said to me is, nobody better than you is going to be there, taking the piss. And he's right. I've now realised that the people that have that much time on their hands to be doing this are people I wouldn't want to be associating myself with anyway, so I simply got a thicker skin, and learnt to laugh it off.

Hotel Shoebox Gym

The issues of the Hotel gym being too small—well, shoebox like, for us—led us to move to our new units at Castle Quay. Whilst negotiating the move, we realised the costs involved, the amount of people or loopholes we had to jump through just to get permission.

We had to get planning permission, and to do that, we need an architect and lawyers.

We had to get all leases signed. We ended up signing up to a 12-year lease. Things were looking good so we were committed. We had a location that was secure and fit for our purpose. We were really excited and looking forward to having a specific location for our training and coaching.

We were in the hub of where everyone wants to be. We were so excited and wanted the building works to commence so that we were ready to move for the 1st of January, 2015 which, made the 90 day goal, and planning the wedding, working over Christmas, my daughter's first Christmas, organising the works etc. was chaotic to say the least.

Absolute rollercoaster

Elly and I got married on Valentine's Day 2015, and went on our honeymoon. The wedding was amazing. Elly had the perfect dress. She looked so beautiful; I married my best friend and the most amazing woman in the world. We had the perfect flowers, the best band, and best of everything. Everything was perfect, just as we had imagined our wedding day to be.

I have to say that ever since Elly and I had our first date, I always knew we were meant to be together, but actually planning the wedding and getting everything perfect for us made it even more clear how much we were meant to be together.

Never once did our opinions clash about anything. Never once did we have a cross wire about it and I know that it's supposed to be a stressful time planning a wedding, but for us it was bliss. Everything just seemed to click, and it was clear that we both had the very same dream. It was perfect. We wanted the same colour theme. We wanted the same people at the wedding. We wanted the same cards, the same everything. There wasn't a single thing out of place, and it was safe to say that our wedding was the perfect wedding for us.

In the build-up to the wedding, Elly and I were closer than ever. One thing that also started to happen was, I started to hear from friends that I hadn't heard of for some time. Probably since I started to run my own business, I was removing myself from as many social situations as I could, you can probably count the true friends I had all the way from setting up my business to this present day in one hand.

However, I did invite more than that to the wedding because you could probably say once again that I was led by my ego on that and decided to invite more and more people so that we could have more people at the wedding to make it even more special, and it was. However, a lesson I learned was, it takes situations like this to realise how far you've drifted away. It's not necessarily a bad thing, but we do drift in life, and I realised I'd drifted away from those people that I call my friends.

We could not fault our wedding day in the slightest. I think everyone had a great day and many of them said it was one of the best weddings they've ever been to. The day after we got married, we jetted off on our honeymoon and had a great two weeks in Mexico. I knew before we went that when I got back, things were going to get much more hectic here because we had our second white-collar boxing event coming up.

I wasn't really looking forward to getting into it, as it means more working hours for 10 weeks solid. However, I was prepared for the long hours starting again. Things got even more hectic when I got a phone call to say that Craig and Kirsty had been rushed to Portsmouth, because they were having complications with their twins, as Kirsty was 20-odd weeks pregnant at the time.

So, getting back and working long hours again, things became really hectic. It's safe to say we didn't really have a honeymoon period after our wedding when we got back and then to make things even worse, one of my colleagues and very good friends, Dean Price, died; he took his own life. I couldn't believe it, the guy who had helped me regain my passion for health and fitness, and he had taken his own life. I couldn't believe I'd never have another chat with him about the most in-depth training things I didn't even fully understand.

I'll never forget the day I received the phone call from my friend, Pascal, late in the evening to tell me. Knocked to my knees, distraught, I didn't sleep that night because I knew I had to put my business head on and start calling his clients the next day to inform them of this terrible news.

It was quite fitting that our white-collar event raised money for Mind Jersey, a local charity that raised money for people suffering with mental health. Something we can only assume my dear friend, Dean Price was suffering from too.

I'll never forget that evening of the white collar when James, who runs Mind Jersey, stood up in front of everyone and presented a speech. I'd never seen so many grown men in tears as I did that night -- when you hear the passion he has when he speaks about mental health and the importance of speaking out when we're suffering.

Something I've always been worried about doing- talking about my mind the thoughts in my head and my struggles. Straight after the white collar, I spoke to Elly about my lack of interest and my unhappiness with operating the business based around money rather than passion.

Dean was one of the people who walked health and fitness around. He wore heart on his sleeve. Everything he did was all about helping people get fitter and healthier and lead a better lifestyle. I actually think he gave me my passion for what I have right now.

Telling people over the phone, I had to try to remain strong while they cried their eyes out over the phone to me. That was by far the most difficult thing I've ever had to do in my life and I can't see anything being harder than that.

I got home that evening after calling up 22 of his clients and telling over 50 members face to face about his death, dropped to my knees, and just burst into tears. I'll never forget Elly; she just put her arms around me, then Aoife-Mae crawled up to me and gave me a cuddle, too. It was the worst feeling in the world.

It's the first time I've ever suffered grief and hope that I'll never have to suffer that again. From then onwards, I completely lost interest in business. I completely -- I started questioning everything. Questioning why we were doing what we were doing and what was the point in everything. It was a very difficult time for me and without Elly; I don't know where I'd be right now.

After Dean died, I became very lost, confused, frustrated, and ultimately a bit angry. Truth be told, I had always thought if someone took their own life, it was an act of selfishness. An act that showed they didn't care about anyone else but themselves.

However, after calming down from a state of anger now, I think it's actually anything but selfish, because at the time they didn't see any other way around things. This really ate me up inside.

I was questioning myself as a person, as his friend, and as his boss, I guess no different from most others that knew him or has been through that kind of loss. Then, I started to realise that I was doing all this stuff and we never know what's around the corner.

I was running the business that I didn't really enjoy running, because I had lost the positive touch with clients, by this I mean, I only heard from them really if something was wrong. I wasn't fulfilling my passion for helping people, I was hiding behind a business because it brought in a good wage. The only passion that I had was to help in coaching people on a personal level, not in a massive group, nor just operating a business managing things.

Shortly after Dean had died, it became clear that both Craig and I have become very distracted and almost a little lost with our lives. We have not only lost a close friend, but also a colleague that was a big part of our business.

Someone who we really knew we could count on and we formed a great relationship with him.

Dean was the first friend that I've ever lost, and I have to say, it was worse than I ever thought it could be. This made me want to sit back and think about my life, and wonder whether what I was doing was really the right thing for me to be doing, to operate a business like this, even though I didn't really have that much of an interest in it.

This is where I really started to question what was going on. I was happily married, had a beautiful daughter and wife, yet I'd spend more time working, and when I wasn't at work, I was thinking or stressing about work, taking me away from spending quality time with my family, and truth is, that was and always is my ultimate goal, to have a lifestyle which meant I could spend that good quality time with my family.

About three to four months after Dean took his own life, we made the tough decision to close one of our locations. To put it in perspective, it was only profiting about £1,500 a month. It was the quietest out of them and therefore the least profitable too. The reason we decided to close the location was because we were setting ourselves up staffing wise. We realised that as soon as someone was on holiday, or someone was sick or more likely someone slept in, Craig and I will have to cover the sessions, and for the modest profits we were making on the location it really wasn't worth the hassle. The truth was, I had no real interest in covering the sessions anymore, as I had completely fallen out of love with it.

When we decided to close the location, we let all the members know, and unfortunately, not many of them stayed on to go to our other locations. This rather reaffirmed my thoughts that at the time, that it really wasn't something I wanted to carry on running, when you consider our next closest location which ran sessions at the exact same time as that one which was just over 5 miles away. It takes about ten minutes to drive from one location to the other at that time in the morning.

The negative, rude emails we received about it really did affect me because they had no idea what was going on in my head and the pressure it was adding to me and my family on top of it. I felt like sending some equally negative, rude emails, but had to bite my tongue and be 'professional.'

New Location Not All it's Cracked Up to Be

Once we had moved locations, we went around and met all of the locals and the businesses on either side of us to make sure that they were happy with us, because of course, we are aware that while we were moving and getting settled, there was going to be an element of noise.

Everything was great. The only person who had any issue was a dentist next door and asked us to move our treadmill, which of course we did to reduce the noise. The business started to grow a little bit, and people started to talk a little bit more and more and we even had other personal trainers, coming in to have a look at what we were doing down there.

Things were good, but that was short lived, after about three months, we had someone from Environmental Health come in to see us. There had been a complaint from the guy next door about the noise that we were making and claimed we were operating a gym.

We had all the right permissions, and we've done all of the correct procedures to make sure that there wasn't too much noise transpiring through, so we thought anyway. Next thing we knew, the bloke from Environmental Health had gone back and reported us for operating a gym, something that we had never done and never would do.

We were operating a small health and fitness studio, where we help people with their health and fitness. In fact, it's safe to say a majority of our clients wouldn't have been comfortable using a gym, which was exactly why we wanted something that was completely different to a gym.

After a few weeks of what seemed like months and many negotiations between our initial architects and the planning department, they decided to issue an enforcement notice, at which time our first architect decided to hold their hands up and say they weren't able to help us any further.

We were in absolute shit street, looking at more sleepless nights, more panic, more worry and money thrown at a problem, felt like we were flogging a dead horse. We called upon an old friend of ours who came in to help us. He was an architect. He helped to keep planning off, and they stopped the enforcement notice. We just had to put in a new planning application to change the use. This planning application requires that we had to put notices to the doors of our units, meaning that we had members deciding they wanted to leave us because of the uncertainty.

It also caused staff members to leave us. After that, our planning application went in front of the panel and was turned down on the grounds of noise. I'll never forget it. I was on holiday, and Craig rang me to tell me the bad news.

He told me that the dentist had stood up and given his account of the noise and read out a letter from a resident from above who'd decided not to attend the meeting. Stressed out, I was panicked and not sure of what to do. This rather resounded my thoughts that I no longer wanted to operate business like this.

When all of these issues with Castle Quay came to the surface, it became clear that we had made another mistake.

I've always been the kind of person who wants everything yesterday. Let's just say I'm far from patient, I want everything done twice the speed that's probably possible.

When it came to negotiating the lease of our units at Castle Quay, we rushed into the first lawyer that we could get hold of and booked him up, then went with him straight away, almost no question asked, apart from how do you want the £2,500 paid.

We really should have done some shopping around with architects and the professionals we used. We went in and used the ones the landlords suggested because they knew the building, took their advice, and unfortunately it didn't pan out right for us.

Once all the issues with environment health and planning all popped up and we were forced to make a change of use. It became very apparent that the people we had employed to do their job didn't quite help us in the way we thought they had.

One of our friends who were in politics was a great help and put us on to a local company called Jersey Business. They were a states funded company that helped businesses and gave them free impartial advice. This was a service Craig and I didn't really have much knowledge about. However, had we known back when we first started, we would have utilised them much more and may not have been in the position we found ourselves in.

My advice to anyone starting a business is to find out locally who can help him or her with the set up and give impartial free advice because it'll be worth it in the long run. The advice that someone outside the business can give is invaluable.

It's amazing how much having somebody who's not in the business and not related to the business can give you so much better advice than you would do yourself. At the time, I also felt that everyone was against us, planning, environmental health, and people spreading rumours. I was ready to throw the towel in an go and get a 'normal' job, if it weren't for Elly reminding me that it was just at the moment I just wasn't doing what my passion was, coaching and it will all be ok in the end.

Unfortunately, I had blinkers on and I knew what I wanted to do and how to go about it. However, I didn't fully understand the implications of the decisions that we were making at the time. The decisions that seemed to be relatively straightforward to us were much more complex.

With lawyers, architects, and other professionals involved, it's crazy how quick the bills can rack up (tens of thousands of pounds). But not only the costs can rack up but times also get delayed because things don't seem to happen as smoothly as someone like myself would expect, and these professionals have to take their time and they won't be rushed, because ultimately their professional reputation is on the line- doesn't ease any frustrations.

Quite simply pissed off now

I'll never forget one day, I was sitting in the car, thinking about the way work was going, about how things were just slipping. I was looking at the things that were happening on a daily basis. Sincerely speaking, things really started to piss me off at the time. Staff were constantly showing up late, not wearing their uniform and drinking a fucking coffee, a fucking coffee, which their clients and I can only assume was why they were late every session. While I was training clients, they were asking where their trainer was session after session; it really irritated me.

I would never stand around drinking a coffee while I'm training a client. I mean these people are paying for coaching and support. Again, I wouldn't constantly turn up late when these people are paying me a small fortune to train with a trainer, and if I was late I at least had the respect for my clients to apologise.

All these frustrations were on the high as I continued seeing these things DAILY. My clients could see my frustrations and disappointment. My clients could see how I feel and it was probably affecting the way I was training them because it really did wind me up. I had to do my best to try and stay as professional as possible without letting them know it was affecting me. And also, without letting it affect them, and the service they were getting from me, even though it did happen.

I looked at it and thought, this is my brand, and this is the brand that I've worked hard to build up. And my frustration started to hit a whole new level. I found it very difficult to try and manage it and this is what started to lead me to decide that I no longer wanted to operate a business like this, pissed off, frustrated, fed up, but with my hands tied.

I was really struggling to cope with it emotionally and physically, because it was winding me up more and more each day.

Shortly after we opened the new Health Clinic at Castle Quay, word had started to go round that Craig and I fell out. Possibly, because Craig was based out of the rock and I was based at Castle Quay.

This was something that we did on purpose to make sure that we could both look after each location and look after the staff who were there. However, this didn't stop the rumours from spreading. One thing that we did realise back then was, if you are doing something right, people are going to talk about you. Therefore, we tried to take it as a positive. However, the rumours seemed to get more and much worse, even malicious and it was coming back to us.

We heard all sorts, even heard that I was moving away with Elly and Aoife-Mae or that Craig, Kirsty and the twins were moving away to the other side of the world too.

We heard all but the one that really frustrated me, was the rumour that Fit Body had gone bust, it was turning over £300k a year yet we had bitter people spreading rumours and it did take an effect on me. It became a very frustrating time for us, but I bit my tongue and carried on, getting on with it. Continuing on this rollercoaster with the business at a good steady, but staff unsettled, issues with planning, and a baby growing into a very hyper toddler.

The Quote 'rumours are carried by haters, spread by fools and accepted by idiots' really comes to mind. Nevertheless, no matter how much it all pissed me off I had to just swallow it up and keep quiet and hope it all passed over.

Elly and I Coaching Together

During the 6 months with the loss of Dean, the trouble with planning, the frustrations with Fit Body Jersey, pretty much everything. I looked at my life and decided that I need to keep my training going. I have to be honest; I was feeling a bit of a fraud this time around telling people about sustainability and not settling when they get to their goal. Yet not doing it myself.

I was telling people how to eat well, and I wasn't doing it myself. I was actually a hypocrite. It was something I had already prided myself in not being. However, it's something I'd become because I decided to chase money, rather than using my passion to help people.

Something I'm not really proud of, but I'm proud to say I've learned from that.

So I decided to focus on my own training, decided to focus on my own diet, and decided to ultimately start practicing what I preach once again.

I've always been one to go on about practicing what I preach although my training methods were completely different to what they are now. Because back then, when I started Fit Body up, I used to box. When I stopped boxing, my training methods completely changed and my beliefs changed on the way training should be done. However, I still had to operate in a business that was still training in a way that I used to do it, and it was me that did that.

I'd begun to a feel a little bit like a hypocrite and I knew that I needed to work on changing that. I started to do a lot less boot camps because that wasn't my style of training anymore and I began to start doing a little bit more one to one training as I could do it how I wanted then.

That was part of what led Elly and me to found Hodgson Fitness, literally practicing what we preach. Delivering it to people online was the best of both worlds for Elly and I. We had more freedom, yet we have to help more people at the same time, just by being ourselves and showing people what we've done, giving them the support, knowledge and guidance that they needed to achieve their goals.

Shortly after doing this, I started to attract more and more people to help them get in better shape, feel better about themselves, and once I started doing that, I was feeling my passion again.

That led me to decide to commit to competing in the body building show.

Therefore, I decided to go and see my friend, Wayne Stewart, who I'd met back from my time in Fitness First. He was smiling, saying that he knew I would want to compete one day. During this time when I started my training, we also had our second white collar build up going on in the background, so I was also working longer hours than I would have liked, again family time suffered.

After I decided to get on stage and compete in the Jersey CI bodybuilding show, I knew that it was going to be tough. I'd done all the sports, such as boxing, running a marathon, middle distance running, and football, even rugby when I was younger. However, nothing was like this. There were no shortcuts, something I knew I would have to stay fully committed to.

When I was in prep for the body building show, I was getting up even earlier, I think sometimes alarm is even set for3:15so that I could get up, start going to work, get my food in me, do my training, and my 'working' day could start. Work was more manic than ever.

Things really weren't the easiest emotionally, I have to say, so all I had to look forward to was a trip to Vegas with our best friends. This was something that kept me going because Katie and Michael had been the two friends that were there for me when I needed them, and they're Aoife-Mae's god parents, Michael was my best friend and they just were the perfect people for us to have a good holiday with.

I went to Vegas and unfortunately broke my hand and wrist in a drunk state, which when I came back made training even harder, and working even harder too.

I had a choice, I was thinking about pulling out of the show, however, like Elly said, I'd worked so hard for the last few months and the last thing I wanted to do was pull out because of this. So I met up with Wayne and discussed this with him and he said I have plenty of time and that I could work around my training because that's the sort of thing I would say to a client, therefore I decided to continue my training, work around it as best as I could, and thankfully the injury didn't hinder me quite as much as I thought it would.

When I was preparing for the body building show, I found it both mentally and physically tough. I was tired with getting up even earlier than normal and it started to really put a pressure on me with work as well because I really wasn't in a happy place with the work side of things.

I did have a slight dream, and it was only a dream of even getting towards, and that was to qualify for the British Championships. However, when I got on stage, I won my category, and got an invite to the British Championships. It was a dream come true for me to achieve this, especially considering this was only my first show, and I was overwhelmed at the thought of it.

As I got that invite to the British, I felt like everything was good again, and falling into place. Fit Body was going pretty well (apart from the planning issues), Hodgson Fitness was going really well and I'd qualified for the British, and adding in that Elly and I started to get more and more people wanting coaching with us. This was something that I hadn't expected to happen through me qualifying particularly as we work mainly with women looking to lose weight. However, it did. It made me really happy and began to realise that Hodgson Fitness was going to be a success too.

This was still getting me down. The only thing I dreaded in my life was going into work to manage people or staff, rather than actually working with clients and helping them towards their weight loss goals. This really made every day seem to drag on and on, as all I was doing was looking forward to getting home and spending a little bit of time with Aoife-Mae and Elly.

For the first time since I started being self-employed, I was clock watching every day. All of our family time together was slowly getting less and less and it was really tough for me, but more so for Elly and Aoife-Mae, but Elly was so supportive.

We did make up for lack of time by having good quality time most days, and we would walk as a family for my cardio. This was all I looked forward to every single evening, spending the two hours or so together before Aoife-Mae went to bed.

The only thing that was in the way now was that Fit Body Jersey was taking up a lot of my time; the running and management of the business I did was dragging my energy levels and my life enjoyment down, when all I wanted to do was actually be personally coaching and helping people. That was something that I really struggled with emotionally because I was in up to my eyes in it with Fit Body and there was nothing I could do about it. I felt trapped doing something I didn't enjoy. This wasn't in the plan; this wasn't in any of the entrepreneur posts, not on any manual to running your own business. The feel was affecting my family time too.

I could flip a switch while I was at work and be 100% ok and on the ball, but putting on an act is tiring, so Elly and Aoife-Mae got tired, fed up, frustrated and out right miserable at me, and everyone else got the happy energetic me. I felt like a bad husband and father for months at the thought of this.

I still had the business that was pretty much getting in the way, eating up time and energy that I could have been spending on either with Aoife-Mae and Elly, or helping grow my coaching business. When Elly and I set up Hodgson Fitness, we were inundated with people wanting to be helped by us.

During this time is when It was extremely clear that I didn't really want anything to do with Fit Body anymore, I did feel well and truly lost. I did feel like I wasn't sure what direction my professional life was going to go in and I even considered if being in the fitness industry was the right thing for me to do with my future.

All I knew was that I had a wife and daughter that I loved and had to provide for. You could say I felt a little bit trapped, doing a job or running a business that didn't give me any satisfaction back. The only thing it gave me was an income and that wasn't to be thrown away

Even when I knew we were going to get rid of Fit Body, I was then still anxious about what happens next. What are we going to do? Even when Hodgson Fitness was gradually building up, there was still always that anxiety that Fit Body was the thing that you could say made me.

Before Fit Body, no one knew who I was. Before Fit Body, I was a nobody, and it's something that worried me and filled me with anxiety every time I thought about it. At this time I had many more sleepless nights thinking about that and how people would perceive it, because the last thing I wanted was for people to perceive it as a negative thing or a greedy thing.

Because it was far from that, in fact, selling Fit Body was probably the hardest decision I have ever made and it's something that I'll always remember because it was such a good three years of my life. It just wasn't going to fit into my life going forward.

Hodgson Fitness got me back going

It became clear that the fit, healthy lifestyle Elly and I were leading became attractive. People knew we were practicing what we preach, and we gained respect from them straight away. Our passion seemed to transfer to our clients. My faith in helping people became restored, working side by side with my wife who has the same passion and thoughts on all things about health and fitness meant we are a perfect team.

Therefore, we decided to really focus on our own online coaching company, Hodgson Fitness. It was quite fitting that a friend of mine, who I'd met on a few events, Dan Meredith decided to set up a group on Facebook called Coffee With Dan around this time.

It was a group that entrepreneurs all work with discussing things on business, holding each other accountable, and it was basically just a lot of fun, but also a lot of learning going on too. It was a really good way to get my passion back and also see that the frustrations I had felt were completely normal. When you drift from relationships, with friends and family, as I had done, you lose touch with what's really going on, and this group really helped me regain touch of it.

This gave us a little bit of a foundation to start and where to start looking when we want to grow on our online company. With no clients, we were looking around on various webinars, pretty much every night, to find answers until we stumbled across our now business coach and friend, AJ Mihrzad.

After watching the webinar and listening to him, you could just sense the passion. You could just believe that he truly wanted to help people which is why we got straight on a call with him and decided that this was the best way forwards for Elly and I with Hodgson Fitness.

I think within the first couple of minutes of the first conversation Elly and I had with AJ, it became very clear that the way that he operated his business was clearly based on passion. He spoke a lot about living life to your true purpose and what you feel is your role in life. He used the term superpower, and we left the phone call energised and excited, it was something we had been missing with our work, excitement.

Even when Elly and I were busy setting up Hodgson Fitness, I think people thought it was an easy process, something that just happened overnight because we kept it pretty quiet to begin with. However, for months, Elly and I spent night after night after Aoife-Mae had gone to bed getting things ready to rock and roll.

We would sit up watching the videos that AJ had sent us to help us get set up, ready to go. We were spending maybe 30 hours a week after Aoife-Mae was in bed to get everything ready from the beginning and that's the reason how it became such a success so quickly.

We have had to put the hours in. I think that's one thing that is inevitable when first setting up a business. You are going to have to work hard behind the scenes to get it off to a good start.

Now Running Hodgson Fitness doesn't really feel like Elly and I are running any sort of business. It feels more like we're just running our lifestyle and operating that in conjunction with our lives.

The reason behind this is that we're running it based on our passion for helping people and we're practicing what we preach. This is the business model I wish I had followed from day one. It's clear that it's not only easier to run from a business point of view, but also people relate to it a lot more because they can see the passion and feel the passion from both of us.

Elly and I both feel we had the same role; our role was to try and help as many people as we can to lead fuller, happier, and healthier lives. So, at this moment, we needed to follow that dream. We need to follow that passion and stop doing things that didn't fit into that. This is a mindset shift that happened immediately for us. It's safe to say that we've never looked back while doing this, because now we feel like we just live our lives and guide people who we deem our friends through the process too.

Selling Fit Body

So I was happy with Hodgson Fitness, and where it was going, I then had to tackle Fit Body, and deciding what to do with it, as it wasn't something I had ever experienced before. Therefore, with a heavy heart I had a chat with Craig about my feelings and thoughts of selling Fit Body Jersey.

After I discussed with Craig my thoughts and feelings about Fit Body, it became clear that he was feeling the same way, he wanted to look at the potential to sell.

It was then that I really was 100% sure that I didn't want to operate a business, it brought me back to when we started out operating the business of Fit Body, and I really just wanted to help people, it reminded me of the reason I first became a personal trainer. I was in PT, mainly because I wanted to help people. Yes of course I wanted to earn good money, but not with all the baggage that comes with what I was getting with Fit Body. I want to help people get in shape, and to make them feel better about themselves, and this was something that I rather lost touch with over the three years of operating Fit Body. This was really what reconsolidated my decision that I no longer wanted to have Fit Body Jersey.

We spoke to one person and then we got an offer pretty much overnight, something we hadn't expected but it made me feel much better about everything pretty much straight away; the thought that I could be freed of this business that was dragging me down emotionally, and wearing me down.

Once we had discussed with the buyers of Fit Body Jersey, finalised the price, the date of takeover, and then there are other things. The planning department came in and spoiled it when it got turned down. It delayed the process and made things a little bit more complicated; meaning that we needed to invest in more lawyers' fees, more architect fees, and ultimately spend a lot more time trying to resolve this and get a deal made, so that Craig and I can move forward and more or less forget about it.

So with the sale, the clients should benefit from having new owners, who are passionate about growing the business and making it even bigger. The staff would benefit, because they would have new bosses in place that would be more motivated to help them get clients, help them stay more motivated to take them on to newer thing.

When planning got turned down, as from the dentists complaints as mentioned earlier (this took months to go through the necessary procedures) rumours started about Fit Body. Rumours started about Craig and I YET AGAIN. You do need thick skin to be in the public eye a bit when operating a business. Questions started being asked. It was a tough decision for us to sell the business; not something we took lightly. It wasn't an easy one, because it did pay the bills at the end of the day and it did bring in good money. Adding to the fact that Craig and I used it as a platform to help one-to-one staff grow too. However, when we looked at it, I realised that as I was running the business, my lack of passion for it was probably clear to the clients (which I now know was).

Shortly after this planning application had been turned down, we had a couple of former members of staff of the dentist next door that came to see us. They came to tell us they hadn't heard anything while they were working there, apart from when we were getting set up in there which was to be expected. They sounded really frustrated and felt terrible that we were in a position where we weren't approved the use of our location despite going through all the necessary procedure prior to starting works in there.

Angry, frustrated and annoyed at hearing this news as we had invested over £120,000 in location, and it was all because somebody had created noise complaints that didn't exist. We were left with no choice but to investigate this further and see what action we could take and the advice to wait until we could quantify the total costs to us before taking it further.

As part of our business sale, because we didn't have planning permission, we have to have a two-staged attack to it where part of the business would be sold and we would remain in the other half of it until the planning issues were resolved.

However, the person who had bought the business was changing the way he operated it slightly, which meant it would fall more under health use, which is something we already have permission to do.

Once we finally had a meeting with the planning, it transpired that the laws have now changed and they would have to re-apply for planning change of use, which was going to incur more fees and take a lot longer than we had planned. This became very clear that the odds were stacked against us even more than we had first imagined. The stress wasn't over, in fact, as this book get published it still isn't over completely although we are a lot further down the line than we were.

The bright side thus far is that I get to spend more time fulfilling my passion, helping people lead healthier lives on a more personal level rather than on a group level. It also means that I get more time to spend with Elly and Aoife-Mae and do stuff together as a family with me actually present rather than with my head in my laptop or on my phone.

Elly has never batted an eyelid, however, it must be tough for her having a husband that's working ridiculous hours, and even when he is home, he's stressed out, fed up, frustrated, and ultimately a little bit angry resenting work.

After selling up

After I sold Fit Body, I made the conscious decision that I was only going to work hours when it suited me. I'd spent the last 3 and a half years putting work before me, my life and more recently Elly and Aoife-Mae and that's embarrassing.

When the announcement was made that I'd sold Fit Body, I was inundated with people contacting me and trying to find out more information. Some being nosey and others being concerned. I think for most people they probably thought I was mad, they couldn't understand why I would sell a profitable business because to them I was living the dream, but my reason was simple.

I would have been mad to keep holding it. I was unhappy, overworked, stressed out, and it was taking time away from Elly and Aoife-Mae, so I would have been even more mad keeping hold of that business that was draining the life out of me. I wanted and still want a life that I can run on my terms, not one that I'm a slave to my job or business.

A few weeks after the sale of Fit Body and I had been contacted by all of these people, it hit me and the shock of them when I described my lack of job satisfaction and the strain it was putting on me.

I was just like those entrepreneurs I had seen a few years back, with the wads of cash, the fancy cars and nice holidays. I was painting the perfect lifestyle; I was painting the happiest life possible, whereas beneath the surface that was far from reality, which was far from the truth. I was a bullshitter.

The truth was; I wasn't happy, I had very little job satisfaction, and I was fed up relying on other people. I wanted to do something that relied only on me, so that's what I was doing. I was following my passion, and that was something that was really important to me, something that I'd sort of lost over the last three years.

I think that's the danger of social media, how easy it is to 'fake' happiness and paint an image that we want people to see. For me it was a strong successful man that was loving life.

Therefore that meant I had to move some of my one-to-one clients to different days or times and if they weren't happy with it, I made myself commit to perhaps lose clients and therefore the income they delivered. Although it might have meant a short-term sacrifice, I hope that in the long-term would be much happier and only be able to work when and how I was happy to work.

Another lesson I learned when dealing with the sale of Fit Body was that you need to make sure that you get everything drawn up, signed off officially by a lawyer, just something legally binding with all the terms included, no matter how big or how small.

Yes, it might cost a few more quid; however, you never know whom you're dealing with. Even if on the surface they seem like really nice people, at the end of the day they're just trying to do the best they can and their word doesn't really mean anything. I experienced this first hand and just a few weeks after the sale had gone through things were changed. This left me pissed off, frustrated and outright annoyed because we felt that we were backed into a corner and we didn't have anything signed off or in writing to give us any sort of meat behind what we thought had been verbally agreed. A costly error from our end. Live and learn

The decision to sell lifted a weight off my shoulders, although I did have to say good-bye to one client I got to say hello to my life again and that's lead me to right now where my passion appears to be stronger than ever.

Right Now

My motivation is stronger than ever. I think working with my wife, Elly, has really made us the dream team. It made me start to appreciate things in life because I'm spending more time with her and Aoife-Mae but I'm also getting to help more people every day.

The mistakes I've made along with the tools AJ gave me, has given me the perfect platform. I think his passion for helping us has really transferred across to Elly and I, which is great.

Elly and I never really envisaged ourselves being as passionate as we are and as concerned as we are about our clients. It's something that I would say to anyone wanting to work for themselves if I could give one bit of advice, the best way to run a business is to run it on passion rather than motivated by money, the shiny object and the 'stuff' you can buy.

Being an entrepreneur is great when it's a people based business and you are 100% your true self because the more people we help, the more we earn; and the other plus side is that by being yourself you attract people you enjoy working with. Truth be told, when starting out, it's really important to make sure the type of clientele you work with, if you could do it for free.

I can't stress the importance of that enough, because if you don't, you'll go down the same road I've been down and then you'll be left with a choice, sell up, carry on but not enjoy it, or start over again, and it's not the easiest thing to decide on. So take your time to work out who you want to work with, and you'll work with them, it may take slightly longer but you will have the 'dream job'.

That's when you know you've got a good business, when you'd happily do your job for free. The money just funds the lifestyle, but the business itself is what drives you. That's when you're not overworking and you're not a slave to the business. For us, we never feel like its work. We always want to help people and we always want to work with these people because they're people that are just like us after self-improvement and need some guidance.

Looking Back

Looking back over these pages, it's clear to see how many bad choices or errors I have made over the last few years, and I can confidently say that I'm very fortunate for the people I have around me because without them, I wouldn't be where I am now.

I have made some tough decisions and I've lost some good friends through running a business, and I also, at one point lost my passion. This is something that I would suggest any person reading this never loses. Maintain your passion. Maintain who you are regardless of anything else.

I think that from operating several small businesses, another thing that I have really learned, the hard way, is that the worst kind of pressure you can be under is the pressure you put on yourself. Pressure to try to succeed and setting targets that are possibly a little bit out of your reach. Having a more levelled approach with a little bit less internal is definitely the way forward to ease the whole process and it takes away any sort of self-doubt because you know you're setting yourself realistic goals. At least then, if you don't achieve them, you should be annoyed with yourself. Rather than setting yourself unrealistic goals, and then being really wound up and frustrated for not achieving them when realistically, it probably was impossible in the first place.

If you start to feel your passions going, you're doing something wrong. You're making the wrong decisions. Taking a step out and looking back in can help you regain that passion. Surround yourself with people on the same journey as you. The same passion as you, which is what I've done by being around Elly and having AJ to coach us has brought the flame in my passion right back, as strong as it has ever been. I'm just glad that I learnt quickly enough that I didn't end up back in a 9-5 job living for the weekend. To maintain that passion and keep moving forward, I've been selective about the people I spend time with, and it has made the world of difference to me, my relationships and my businesses.

I've also found that by having this passion, I've gained more committed and more passionate clients myself. Again, it's that typical story of being yourself attracts longer way around than it needed to be.

You can spend hours and hours preparing a business plan, to get your shit together, so you hit the ground running when you start a business. When you actually get to starting and setting up a business. However, I believe that no amount of planning can fully prepare you for what the world is going throw at you.

You never really know what's around the corner. The truth is that all you can do is focus on doing the best you can, at the time and try and be one step ahead. So once you start building momentum getting systems and procedures in place that work for you to make running it smooth then hopefully you'll be able to deal with things a little better than I have done over the last three years. I mean it dealt with them ok, but I think I had a lot more stress put on me because I was always trying to predict the future, the term, READY FIRE AIM comes to mind.

Then again, when you have a business that you are running on passion, things will run much smoother and there will be no major pressures because you will love what you do. You can outsource the stuff you do not like.

It's really clear that people more often than not underestimate the importance of having a good support network of people around you. It's safe to say that if I didn't have the support of family at the beginning and the support of friends, I probably wouldn't be where I am now. In fact, I definitely wouldn't be where I am and then moving forward, having the support of wife and daughter, even as things got even more and more demanding and they were almost side-lined, never once did they question it, they just supported me.

You can only go so far on your own and you do need people around you to hold you up, to keep you motivated, and generally just keep you going. That is probably the most important thing to have around you when you first set up because it is going to be tough and if it's not tough, you're probably not doing it right.

Since selling Fit Body to get me more time to spend good quality time with Elly and Aoife-Mae, because truth be told, although I have always spent a lot of time at home with them, I wasn't actually present. I spent more time looking at my phone, reading e-mails, and stressed out constantly on edge, waiting for the phone to go for someone to call in sick or for someone to be complaining about something, and it stressed me out.

I've managed to spend more, better quality time with them. I've also been able to dedicate more time to coaching with Elly and my Coaching clients. This has relieved so much stress for me and I'm fulfilling my passion, as well as generating a good income, instead of just generating a good income and finding my passion slowly slipping away, sapping the life out of me.

Right now, I'm still getting some help and counselling from Mind Jersey who have really helped me over the last few months of my own mental/psychological battles, which I have struggled with and struggled to understand why too.

I think the stresses and pressures of running and operating a few successful, yet demanding businesses in such a short space has all really taken its toll on me upstairs. Pair that with having a family and I know what I should have been doing, and I am certain I haven't been doing it.

I have to say now that I am getting counselling, I can appreciate the benefits from doing this. It was something that in my head, I had always thought was only for people who are weak, or only for people who couldn't quite handle things.

However, it's not that at all. It's actually a sign of strength because I admitted that I did need help and still do. I need help to cope with things mentally because for some reason, I was stuck -- I was trying to burn a candle at both ends. The counselling has helped me realise that I need to put my family and me first because life's too short.

I have found that difficult to deal with emotionally. I'm so confident that now I can start dedicating more quality, undistracted time to my family and still operate a successful business, which is what I am doing right now.

When people talk about health, we often think about physical health, because it's something we can see. For example, if somebody's in good shape, toned up, looks fit and athletic, we'll assume they're healthy.

However it's a shame, we often forget about mental health, and that's something that I think can have a big impact on entrepreneurs and small business owners, because of the mental strain that we put ourselves under, trying to develop and operate our own business.

Like I've said previously in this book, you have to do everything. There's a lot of pressure on you to deliver, it's all coming from all angles, and ultimately there's no guarantees you're going to make money. You don't have a contract that says you will be paid for a certain number of hours a week. You basically have to work until you earn enough and keep working to keep building and retain your clients.

So mental health is something that I think should really be brought to mind and really be thought about when you are setting up on your own. In addition, it's not weak to ask for help.

Never worry about asking for help, we all need it from time to time whether that is physical help, or just some help mentally.

When you look at what I've done over the last three years, it's clear to see that most people only really see the beginning and the end. They just see people who have got 'stuff' wads of cash, fancy cars and nice holidays.

They have the 'shiny objects' that they wished they have but they don't see all of the hard work that goes into it behind the scenes. They don't see the stress levels, they don't see the sacrifice, and they don't see the level of commitment acquired to get the things. It's safe to say now that my respect for people who are where I want to be has increased tenfold.

I know the work that I'm going to have to do is going to be even harder moving forward. However, I'm confident that I'll get there. I'm lucky that now I've found myself in a position where the business I operate is more on my terms with compared to a business that's just going to make money, it's a business that will make me money and run under my terms.

Not on terms governed by others, nor is it reliant on others either, it's just reliant on Elly and I. That's the one biggest thing I think I've learned over the last three years since becoming an entrepreneur; start it on your terms and keep it that way. Yes, the growth may be slower, however it'll be long lasting and you'll live a much happier stress free life.

Since being self-employed, it's safe to say that my whole priorities have changed. I first became self-employed because I wanted to do what I wanted when I wanted, and how I wanted to do it.

I had the feeling that I was just going to be free, and be able to only do things that suited me not fully recognising the background work that goes into setting up, owning and running your own business. I guess it was easier being single setting up the business because I could dedicate the time and make it my priority all the way through, it was just I didn't change my priorities as quickly as I would have liked when Elly and Aoife-Mae came into my life.

However, now my priorities have changed. My priority is now being a good father and husband to Elly and Aoife-Mae, because now that's really all I want to do. I want to be a good role model for them, and I want to be the man that they look up to and can rely on, no matter what.

Therefore, I do still have ambition. I do want to continue to grow to both help more people, and to provide a good life for me and my family. Which I feel I am doing now.

Bear This in Mind

This really shouldn't come across as if working for yourself shouldn't be done, because I think if you've got the ambition to do it, then you shouldn't put it off. I just think it's important that we are aware that it's not easy, you have to become the business, you have to do the job, you have to deliver the service, you have to market, and you have to book-keep.

You have to basically do everything: you have to do your accounts, the tax return, and everything all pulls into it. You have to manage it, and if you don't do it yourself, you have to find someone to do it for you and of course when starting out, you may not have the money. Ultimately, it's all your responsibility. The harder you work, the more you earn though, so it is very rewarding. I think if we can all go into it with our eyes open to the behind the scenes area of it working in the business, we'll be much better entrepreneurs.

Another thing to be aware of when starting your journey to the world of being an entrepreneur is that you can have all the friends in the world, feel really popular, have thousands of people on Facebook, thousands of followers on Instagram, and still feel like the loneliest person in the world. And sometimes, being on the entrepreneurial journey, that's the way it can feel. I've felt like that quite often throughout my journey.

I've felt like the only people I've had have been Elly and Aoife-Mae, completely self-inflicted. Nevertheless, it is still hard because people don't get it. People see you painting this perfect picture, and it really isn't like that sometimes, the long hours, the late nights, the loss of social contact can get tough. They can be hard, but you have to persevere if that's what you want because otherwise there was no benefit to that sacrifice if you just give up.

Right now Elly and I are working on a few different things, one of them being a new partnership, with a friend we've networked with, Harry Zambon. We plan to do some escapes where we'll be taking people on a seven day journey to help them improve their mind set and help ultimately get more balance in their lives, so that they can feel less stressed and generally happier.

We plan to arm them with more coping mechanisms that we've learned through our experiences over the last few years. This is something that I'm really excited about, and it's going to give me the opportunity to work face to face with people as I've slowly moved away from that, bit by bit.

At the start of your journey?

When starting out to be self-employed, it's important to be ready for a bumpy ride. The last five years or so since I started working for myself have been an absolute roller coaster. There's been really, really big highs; also some really, really big lows. I've learned that as long as you can learn from the lows, you can create more highs and avoid as many lows, then you're in for a good ride and it will be enjoyable and the rewards will be worth it.

We should always try to keep things as simple as we possibly can and only really work within what we know. Of course, with that I'm still a big believer in trying to improve your knowledge and increase your range of skills or capabilities.

However, if something is out of your comfort zone, or you're spending time on something not being productive, you're better off trying to outsource it. That way you can work on other things that are going to be some of best quality, without you having to stress out about doing it, and perhaps letting your standards drop.

Because when you're running your own business and being an entrepreneur, you are your brand, you are your everything. Therefore, it's really important to make sure the things you all do are done to a high standard.

If I were to give you 3 vital tips when starting out your own business, the first one would be do your homework. Do your homework about your chosen industry, about setting up a business, about accounts, about the support that's out there, about the free advice you could get.

Do as much research as you can before you do anything else. Don't start going into it without doing the research it may take a little longer but it'll deliver for you in the long run.

The second tip is, be prepared to work for free. It sounds somewhat crazy, but at the start, you have to invest a lot of time and effort and get very little in return. Sometimes it's very frustrating as it did in my case, frustrating and very demoralising at times- however, if you have the right product and the business, with time, income will build up very quickly.

The third tip is without a doubt the most important to me; never give up. There are going to be times that it gets difficult, there are going to be times when you'll feel like throwing in the towel and giving it all up, and going back to working in the job you hated.

In fact, I've lost count of the number of times I've thought about throwing the towel in. However, you've done the hard work, you've got a business, you're running it, it's just challenging at the moment. However, what business, or what job, doesn't have challenges with it? Eventually the hard work will pay off.

I think I'll close by saying when running a business, mindset is everything. We have to remain positive because unfortunately when you do well, there's always going to be the negative people or the negative things that can happen and if we dwell on it too much, it can get us down and stop us from fulfilling our passions of being self-employed and working for ourselves, operating a business based on passion.

So we do need to have that positive mental attitude and a can-do attitude so that no matter what comes up to us we'll be able to face it and go through it because you've done the hardest step by deciding to be self-employed, something a lot of people don't take the risk to do.If you do it properly, you can live a life that you can really enjoy.

So go out there and take your stake on the world, and thank you for reading this book.

I hope you can take something away from it and become the success you deserve to be. I really want to help as many people as I can.

Thank You

I fear that often that appreciation isn't given out as much as it should be

And it's something I've noticed first hand since being in the fitness industry, and it's something that pisses me off because we all have people who help us on the way to where we are today. I think it's only fair that I show appreciation to the people that have helped me and supported me on my journey since I first started, all those years ago back in Fitness First.

The Sales Manager

I do owe a massive thank you to the sales manager when I was at Fitness First. She really helped me to grow my business and increase my confidence to keep building my client base. Without her, helping me at the time, I may have ended up going back to the job that I hated, and that's something that I am eternally grateful for. It was one of them things where it was a difficult decision to remove her job role from our company and an extremely tough decision. But I will always remember the help and support she gave me when I first started, and help was hard to come by.

Paul Mort

I certainly owe a big thank you to Paul Mort, who's helped me while I had Fit Body. He helped me to grow our business week on week to what it was when we sold it. I think without Paul giving us the confidence to be ourselves 100% of the time and do what we really wanted I would've still been running that business absolutely hating it. Fed up, Frustrated, down right pissed off. So I am thankful for that.

Craig Culkin

My business partner and friend of 3 years and counting (still have the Rock) is someone I am extremely grateful to have in my life. Craig has been by my side since we started and we have stuck together every step of the way. We've been through some tough times and made some tough decisions, but our relationship has never really been questioned. We've stayed solid and supported each other no matter what we've faced, and that's something that I'll always be grateful for. I've not only got a business partner in him. I've got a good friend, too.

AJ Mihrzad

Now a HUGE thank you to AJ Mihrzad for the help and support that he's given me since Elly and I started Hodgson Fitness which has grown pretty much daily since he took us under his wing. It's safe to say, without him giving me/us that help, that push, that nudge and that knowledge, I would never be where I am now. I'd probably still be running Fit Body Jersey and ultimately not fulfilling my passion, counting down the minutes, seconds, hours to the weekend, but that's not the case now. I now have a job, a role in a business that I absolutely love doing, and that's all thanks to him, which is why I asked him to do the foreword on this book. This man has not just become my mentor but a true friend to me throughout a tough last 8 months and his positivity and motivation has literally kept me growing Hodgson Fitness.

My Beautiful wife Elly

Of course I owe the biggest thank you to Elly for her continued support throughout the last three years of me running and operating the Fit Body Jersey. It can't have been easy for her often having to take a back seat, to business, to work, and ultimately have to understand the fact that I was operating a business that was more demanding than what it should've been. And for that I will never forget and I'm eternally grateful for it. I know that now we're in a position that we can enjoy the rest of our lives running our business together in the future. All based on our passion that was the thing that brought us together. I couldn't do it without her.

There are many other people I could go on and thank but fear it would probably bore the shit out of you, that and you have a life to go and lead on YOUR terms.

My Mum

I would like to extend a special thank you to my mum because, without doubt, the work ethic that I have is from her. She has always worked extremely hard and been the perfect role model for me to learn what hard work is all about. She's had various different jobs and now has a successful career in human resources.

I would appreciate your feedback and 5 stars rating on Amazon; I personally read each review.

Ryan Hodgson